D1481829

Grateful Dead

"What a Long, Strange Trip it's Been"

Michele C. Hollow

Enslow Publishers, Inc.
40 Industrial Road
Box 398
Berkeley Heights, NJ 07922
USA
http://www.enslow.com

REBELS OF ROCK

...ck Library
9 South Broadway
...ack, NY 10960-3834

To Steven,
For making this long strange trip so magical.
-Michele

Copyright © 2009 by Michele C. Hollow

All rights reserved.

No part of this book may be reproduced by any means without the written permission of the publisher.

Library of Congress Cataloging-in-Publication Data

Hollow, Michele C.
Grateful Dead: "what a long, strange trip it's been" / Michele C. Hollow.
p. cm.—(Rebels of rock)
Summary: "A biography of American folk rock band Grateful Dead"—Provided by publisher.
Includes bibliographical references (p.), discography (p.), and index.
ISBN-13: 978-0-7660-3028-2 (library ed.)
ISBN-10: 0-7660-3028-8 (library ed.)
1. Grateful Dead (Musical group)—Juvenile literature. 2. Rock musicians—United States—Biography—Juvenile literature. I. Title.
ML3930.G735H65 2009
782.42166092'2—dc22 [B]
2007041916

032010 Lake Book Manufacturing, Inc., Melrose Park, IL

Nyack Library
59 So... ...way
Nyack, ...0-3834

ISBN-13: 978-0-7660-3620-8 (paperback)
ISBN-10: 0-7660-3620-0 (paperback)

Printed in the United States of America

10 9 8 7 6 5 4 3 2

To Our Readers: We have done our best to make sure all Internet Addresses in this book were active and appropriate when we went to press. However, the author and the publisher have no control over and assume no liability for the material available on those Internet sites or on other Web sites they may link to. Any comments or suggestions can be sent by e-mail to comments@enslow.com or to the address on the back cover.

Every effort has been made to locate all copyright holders of material used in this book. If any errors or omissions have occurred, corrections will be made in future editions of this book.

♻ Enslow Publishers, Inc., is committed to printing our books on recycled paper. The paper in every book contains 10% to 30% post-consumer waste (PCW). The cover board on the outside of each book contains 100% PCW. Our goal is to do our part to help young people and the environment too!

Photo Credits: Associated Press, pp. 4, 64, 69, 79, 86; Boston Globe/Barry Chin/Landov, p. 62; Charles Gatewood/The Image Works, p. 8; Clayton Call/Redferns, pp. 42–43; dgans/flickr, pp. 52, 84; Everett Collection, p. 15; GAB Archives/Redferns, pp. 22, 37; Getty Images, pp. 46, 66; Herb Greene, p. 34; Landov, p. 59; Photofest Digital Library, p. 10; Pictorial Press Ltd., p. 20; Reuters/David Rae Morris/Landov, p. 55; WireImage/Getty Images, p. 74–75.

Cover Photo: Associated Press. (Members of the Grateful Dead in the 1970s.)

CONTENTS

Deadheads are among the most generous people. Thanks for your stories and enthusiasm. Thanks to Dennis McNally, publicist with the Grateful Dead, for sharing his insights. Billy Procida and Michael Beckerman opened doors so I could meet Bob Weir; thanks to Bob Weir for taking the time to chat with me. David Gans was also eager to share information—thank you.

Thanks to Barry Askew for sharing a stack of Grateful Dead photographs and newspaper articles—making my research a lot easier. And thanks to my wonderful editor at Enslow.

Seven hundred fifty thousand people attended the rock festival

1

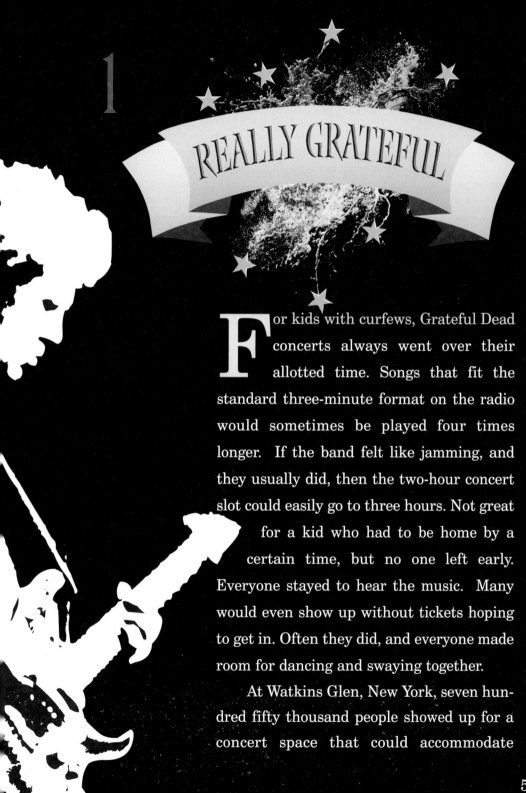

REALLY GRATEFUL

For kids with curfews, Grateful Dead concerts always went over their allotted time. Songs that fit the standard three-minute format on the radio would sometimes be played four times longer. If the band felt like jamming, and they usually did, then the two-hour concert slot could easily go to three hours. Not great for a kid who had to be home by a certain time, but no one left early. Everyone stayed to hear the music. Many would even show up without tickets hoping to get in. Often they did, and everyone made room for dancing and swaying together.

At Watkins Glen, New York, seven hundred fifty thousand people showed up for a concert space that could accommodate between one hundred thousand and one hundred fifty thousand. This was the summer of 1973; concert organizers paired the Grateful Dead with the Allman Brothers Band. The site of the concert was the Grand Prix racetrack arena, which was often filled to capacity with race-car fans. The rest of the time, this picturesque sleepy town in the Finger Lakes region has a population of a little more than twenty-one hundred.

Just two weeks before the Saturday, July 27 concert, one hundred thousand tickets were sold. Tickets were just ten dollars each.

Concert organizers and Watkins Glen officials had to make sure there was enough room to accommodate the crowds. Concert organizers and town officials installed 1,000 portable toilets, added 200 acres of parking, hired 500 state cops and 135 drug abuse control officers, and employed pilots to fly three choppers overhead. The town spent thirty thousand dollars for fencing around the racetrack. They also had to make sure there was enough food and water for one hundred fifty thousand people.

Three days before the concert, fifty thousand people camped outside the arena. The day before the concert, two hundred thousand people showed up. Traffic in and out of Watkins Glen was impossible to maneuver. The promoters briefly thought about refunding everyone's money. Then more people arrived.

On the day of the concert, seven hundred fifty thousand people lined the streets from the doors of the arena to a two-mile radius.

Members of the Grateful Dead were truly grateful to their fans for showing up in droves. To enable the audience to hear, they had their crew fly in McIntosh amplifiers, which weighed 125 pounds each, and two sets of sound-delay towers.

Because of the large number of people lining the roads, members of the Grateful Dead couldn't drive or walk to their gig. Instead, a helicopter dropped Jerry Garcia, Bob Weir, Phil Lesh, Mickey Hart, Bill Kreutzmann, and Vince Welnick onto the stage. It was a heavenly entrance, causing a lot of cheers and excitement from their fans.

Those who couldn't get a seat inside the racetrack found seats in trees, on cars, on the fence, and wherever there was space. Jane Healy (name has been changed), a fan who traveled from New Jersey, got a seat inside the arena. "It was tight," she says. "Not a lot of room for us to sway and dance. Yet, it was electric—so much excitement."[1]

Concerned for the safety of the audience in the sweltering summer heat, a few crew members got into a water truck and doused the crowd. The crowd showed their appreciation by cheering. The cool water was like a welcome rain shower on a hot summer's day.

PEOPLE HELP CLEAN UP AFTER THE FESTIVAL.

"They put on a good show," says Healy. "The Allman Brothers were good. But we were there for the Grateful Dead. Watching Jerry [Garcia] play is amazing."[2]

The county sheriff was quite impressed with the peaceful crowd. He told a local newspaper that there were five times as many people at this concert than at the auto races that are typically held at the arena, and they were getting less than half the trouble. He added that overall, these kids were on their best behavior.[3]

With seven hundred fifty thousand in attendance at Watkins Glen, the majority of the audience didn't pay because there was no way possible to collect money from everyone. "That didn't bother the members of the Grateful Dead," says Dennis McNally, their publicist for twenty plus years. "Performing wasn't about the money. They played in small venues, clubs, college campuses, and large arenas. They loved playing to live audiences."[4]

The Grateful Dead in the mid-1960s

2

A BAND WITHOUT A LEADER

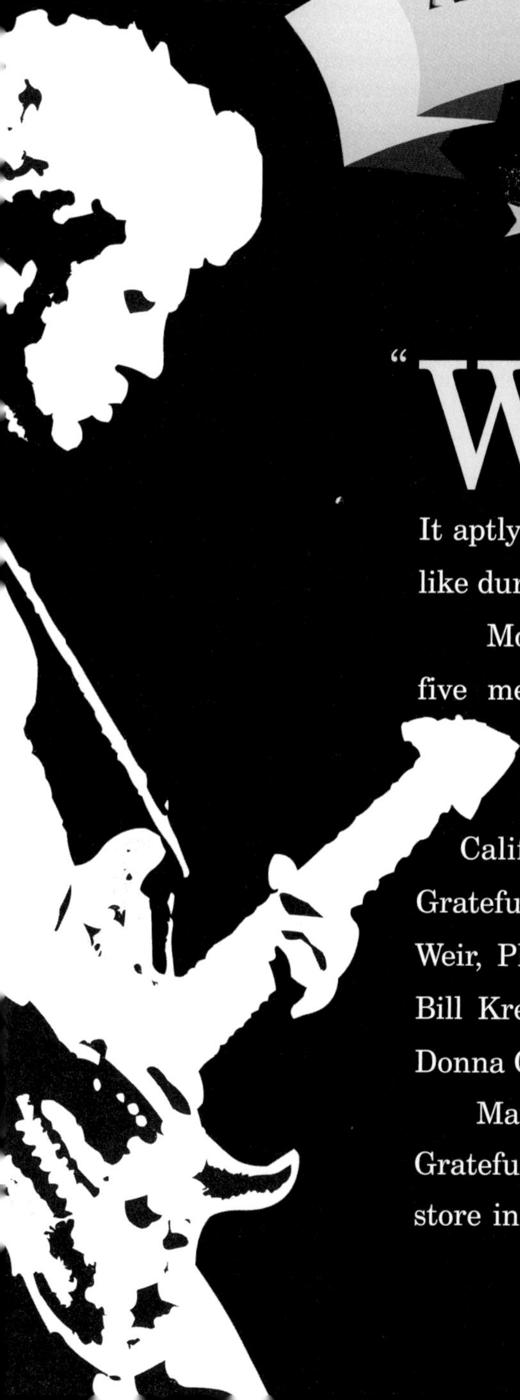

"What a long strange trip it's been" comes from the classic Grateful Dead song "Truckin'." It aptly describes what life on the road was like during the band's thirty-year span.

Most rock bands are made up of four or five members—the Grateful Dead had a dozen members over the years. Formed in 1965 in San Francisco, California, the key members of the Grateful Dead included Jerry Garcia, Bob Weir, Phil Lesh, Ron "Pigpen" McKernan, Bill Kreutzmann, Mickey Hart, Keith and Donna Godchaux, and Brent Mydland.

Many of the principal members of the Grateful Dead met at Dana Morgan's music store in Palo Alto, California, a little south of San Francisco. It was here that Garcia bought a banjo from a teenage employee named Bill Kreutzmann, who later became the drummer and an original member of the Dead. A few weeks later, Garcia was working at the store and performing in a number of bluegrass bands. Here he also met Bob Weir, lead singer, songwriter, lead guitar player, and founding member of the Dead. Ron "Pigpen" McKernan, a founding member who played keyboards, harmonica, percussion, and guitar, also hung out at Dana Morgan's music store. Robert Hunter, lyricist, frequented the store too.

Garcia, Hunter, Weir, Kreutzmann, and McKernan formed a group called Mother McCree's Uptown Jug Champions. They played bluegrass music, and the sound kept on changing. Later it moved to a more electric rock and roll sound. Embracing more eclectic sounds, Mother McCree's Uptown Jug Champions evolved into the Warlocks, which morphed into the Grateful Dead. "One of the reasons the music kept on changing was due to our interests and our love of all different forms of music," says Bob Weir.[1]

Jerry Garcia

Jerry Garcia never wanted to be the leader of the Grateful Dead. "It wasn't that he didn't want to take charge, he just wanted all decisions to be decided on by every member of the band," says Dennis McNally, the band's publicist.[2]

In most groups, the leader is often the lead singer/songwriter—the one who manages and makes most of the major decisions for the band. "Members of the Dead decided everything by vote," says McNally. "It was a democracy—not a ruling by one member."[3]

However, when fans are asked about the Grateful Dead, Jerry Garcia's name instantly comes to mind. It is synonymous with the Grateful Dead. While he didn't want the title or burden of leading the Grateful Dead, Garcia was the founder, lead guitarist, and lead singer of the group.

Born August 1, 1942, Jerry Garcia was named Jerome John Garcia after Jerome Kern, an American composer of popular music in the first half of the twentieth century. Both of his parents loved music. Jerry's father, whom he was close to, was a swing musician. When Jerry was five years old, his dad died. "He was fishing in one of those rivers in California, like the American River," Garcia says. "We were on vacation, and I was there on the shore. I actually watched him go under. It was horrible. I was just a little kid, and I didn't really understand what was going on, but then, of course, my life changed. It was one of those things that afflicted my childhood. I had all my bad luck back then, when I was young and could deal with it."[4]

Another childhood trauma happened that same year during a camping trip. His brother Clifford was chopping wood for a campfire and accidentally chopped off a part of Jerry's middle finger, right below the first knuckle. Once the bandages were removed, Garcia realized a major part of his finger was gone. He says, "But after that, it was okay, because as a kid, if you have a few little things that make you different, it's a good score. So I got a lot of mileage out of having a missing finger when I was a kid."[5]

While his mom and grandparents treated him with lots of love, they didn't allow him to use this trauma as a means to get out of things he didn't want to do. His mom made him take formal piano lessons, which he really didn't want to do. He longed to play the guitar. But at age nine, he started playing piano.

When he turned fifteen, he was given an accordion from his mom, a gift he didn't want. He convinced her to exchange it for a Danelectro guitar that he saw hanging in a pawnshop window in a store in his native San Francisco. The guitar was the perfect instrument for him; he took to it instantly and practiced every waking minute. "I was just beside myself with joy," he said. "I started banging away on it without having the slightest idea of anything. I didn't know how to tune it up.

I never took any lessons. I don't even think there was anybody teaching around the Bay area. I mean electric guitar was like from Mars, you know. You didn't see 'em even."[6]

When he first picked up the guitar in 1957, rock and roll was just beginning to come into popularity. Garcia listened to swing, folk, country, jazz, rhythm and blues, classical, and popular music. "I've always been really fond of folk music; I've always

JERRY GARCIA IN THE MID-1960S

been fond of the fragment," he says. "The song that has one verse. And you don't know anything about the characters, you don't know what they're doing, but they're doing something important. I love that. I'm really a sucker for that kind of song."[7]

Shortly after learning the guitar, Garcia picked up the banjo and started strumming it. He would often switch from guitar to banjo at many of his concerts. Playing banjo and guitar didn't come easy to him—even though it looked effortless. He constantly practiced and didn't let an old injury stop him either.

Art was also an integral part of Garcia's life. He produced more than five hundred works of art during his lifetime. Garcia was extremely bright, but he didn't like school. He dropped out of high school and enlisted in the army in 1958. He was stationed at Fort Winfield Scott in San Francisco. Garcia completed basic training and service school training as an auto mechanic.

Garcia's time in the army was brief. Less than a year after enlisting, he was discharged from the army after accruing two court-martials and eight AWOLs (Absent Without Official Leave). He had trouble following the regime and strict army guidelines. So, with guitar in hand, he headed back home to San Francisco looking for ways to professionally play and write music.

At this time, he enrolled in the Art Institute in San Francisco to study painting for a short time, then gravitated to the coffeehouse scene, where musicians would perform, near Stanford University back in Palo Alto.

He spent most of his time at Stanford University where he met Robert Hunter, songwriter and poet. Garcia and Hunter formed the Thunder Mountain Tub Thumpers, a bluegrass band.

In 1963, Jerry Garcia married Sara Ruppenthal. They had one daughter named Heather. They divorced in 1967. In 1981, he married Carolyn Adams, and they had two daughters, Annabelle and Theresa. Adams and Garcia divorced in December 1987. He had a fourth daughter named Keelin with partner Manasha Matherson in 1987, while he was still married to Carolyn Adams. In 1994, he married Deborah Koons. Those who knew Garcia said that Koons and music were the loves of his life.

Later, Garcia's marriage problems seemed to have stemmed from his love of music and later his battle with drugs. He spent more time practicing, playing, and touring with the members of the band than with his family. He experimented with LSD and other popular drugs of the time. The one drug that had the most damaging effect was heroin. He tried to give up drugs on numerous occasions. "Drug use, is kind of a dead end street," says Garcia. "It's one of those places you turn with your problems, and pretty soon all your problems just become that one problem. Then it's just you and the drugs."[8]

Robert Hunter

Robert Hunter was born Robert Burns on June 23, 1941, in San Luis Obispo, California. He and Jerry Garcia played together in a handful of bluegrass bands in the 1960s. One of the better known bands was called the Tub Thumpers. Hunter played mandolin and upright bass.

Throughout the long career of the Grateful Dead, Hunter wrote the lyrics for the majority of the Grateful Dead's songs. Playing next to Garcia in the Tub Thumpers, just merely fooling around at local college campus gigs or performing at coffeehouses that had open microphones and stages, it was apparent that Garcia was the stronger of the two musicians. Hunter was known affectionately as the member of the Grateful Dead who never came out onstage with the group because he wrote the majority of the lyrics and resided with the group when they lived in the Haight Ashbury section of San Francisco.

Hunter performed less and less with Garcia. However, he wrote more and more. When it came to songwriting, Garcia was a perfectionist and Hunter's lyrics were a perfect match for Garcia's music. Hunter proved to be a great songwriter. He wrote some of the Grateful Dead's most memorable songs, including "Truckin'," "Dark Star," "Sugaree," "Sugar

Magnolia," and the 1987 hit "Touch of Grey," which was the Grateful Dead's only top ten single. In 1974, Hunter began recording solo albums on the Dead's record label. Hunter has a distinctive soothing voice.

Bob Weir

Bob Weir, born October 16, 1947, in San Francisco, California, had a lot in common with Garcia and the other members of the Grateful Dead. They all started fiddling with different instruments at a young age. Weir, the lead singer, guitar player, and songwriter, started playing piano at age nine. "I later switched to the trumpet and then the guitar," he says. "My parents were happy with the guitar because it wasn't as loud."[9]

As a child, music didn't come easy to Weir. "It didn't have to," says Weir, who started playing guitar in 1960 at age thirteen. "If you want to do something because of the love of it, it will happen. Playing well took a lot of practice, but it was something I wanted to do."[10]

Weir excelled in and enjoyed playing sports and making music. He had some difficulty in school due to undiagnosed dyslexia, a learning disability. "With music, I had a stick with it attitude because I loved it and still do," he explains. "I liked and still like listening to all kinds of music—classical, R&B, rock and roll, world music, everything."[11] Weir credits his brother with instilling the love of music in him: "When I was little, my older brother showed me how to tune a radio, and I

Bob Weir

was hooked on music. At the time, I wasn't old enough to perceive music as a fashion statement. I didn't associate myself with any kind of music. I liked it all, and that was what I enjoyed about being a part of the Grateful Dead; we all shared the same philosophy when it came to music. We were all open to listening to, learning about, and experimenting with different forms of music."[12]

Weir continued, "We rehearsed often, and established a kind of wordless communication. When you have a common bond—which for us was the music—you become tight with one another. Blood is thicker than water, and what we had was thicker than blood."[13]

Weir was the youngest member of the Grateful Dead. He was with them from the start of his musical career. In 1975, when the Grateful Dead took a break from touring and recording, he toured and recorded with a number of groups, including Kingfish and Bobby and the Midnites.

After the Grateful Dead dissolved in 1995, Weir formed Ratdog Revue, which was shortened to Ratdog. He leads Ratdog and tours often.

Phil Lesh

Original Grateful Dead member Phil Lesh, who was born on March 15, 1940, in Berkeley, California, jokes that he learned to play bass guitar on the job. He started out playing trumpet at age fourteen in 1954.

Phil Lesh

Influenced by jazz greats John Coltrane and Miles Davis, Lesh enrolled at UC Berkeley to become a music major. He and his friend, Tom Constanten, a keyboardist with the Dead for two years, were turned off by UC Berkeley's music department. Lesh and Constanten understood the importance of learning classical music, but felt that the music department stifled individual creativity. Halfway through his first semester, Lesh dropped out. He enrolled in Luciano Berio's class at Mills College. Berio, an Italian composer of classical and electronic music, had a deep interest and appreciation for experimental sounds. Berio encouraged Lesh to compose his own music. The two formed a tight connection centered around music.

After Berio's class, Lesh took a job as an engineer at a local radio show. He attended a concert at Kepler's bookstore in Palo Alto, California. Here he heard Garcia and Ron "Pigpen" McKernan play in a band they put together called the Warlocks. Impressed with their performance, Lesh invited them to play on the radio show, and soon a friendship formed.

One night in 1965, Lesh, Garcia, Pigpen, and Weir attended a party in Palo Alto. At the party, Lesh told Garcia that he wanted to play an electric instrument—possibly bass guitar. At the Warlocks next concert, Lesh was asked to come up onstage and play. He was invited back, and that is how he "learned on the job."

"He is credited with adjusting the bass so that it was louder and had a richer sound," says McNally.[14] Prior to this, bass players were basically timekeepers—keeping the beat of the song. At each Grateful Dead concert, Lesh would improvise a solo for himself. One of the best improvisations he created was with the hit song "Dark Star."

Bill Kreutzmann

Bill Kreutzmann, born May 7, 1946, in Palo Alto, California, started playing drums at age eight. He was the drummer and original member of the Grateful Dead. As a young child, he played drums at his mom's dance class, improvising and keeping his own beat. He always had a fondness for the drums. When he was twelve, he got a paper route to pay for his first drum set. "I saw a drummer play once when I was a kid and I thought, that's really cool," he says. "You know, you're moving. You're using your arms and fingers. So I tried it and I loved it."[15]

Formalized music classes in grade school didn't go as well as the performances at his mother's dance class. He got kicked out of his grade school's band; his teacher kept telling him he couldn't keep a beat. That didn't deter him. The determined young Kreutzmann took private lessons and would practice again and again. As a teenager in Palo Alto, he formed a handful of rock bands including the Wildwood Boys and the Legends.

He met Garcia at Dana Morgan's music store, where he sold him a banjo. In 1963, Kreutzmann formed a band called the Zodiacs. The Zodiacs featured Ron "Pigpen" McKernan on harmonica and Garcia on bass. When they began playing electric instruments in 1965 they dubbed themselves the Warlocks, but finding the name already in use, they thumbed through a dictionary until they stumbled on "grateful dead, defined as a traditional British folk ballad in which a person helps a ghost who has recently died find peace."[16]

Mickey Hart

Mickey Hart, who was born on September 11, 1943, in Brooklyn, New York, loves all things related to drums. While he was attending elementary school, Hart convinced his mom to sign him up for drum lessons. Drums were the central focus of his life. "There's nothing like music to relieve the soul and uplift it," he says.[17]

A loner, Hart excelled at playing the drums. He would often retreat to the garage of his house to practice. Playing the drums allowed Hart to escape childhood troubles. His father left home when Hart was young, so he was raised by his mom. When he was a teenager, his mother remarried and they moved to Cedarhurst, Long Island, in New York. In his senior year, he left school to join the air force, where he was stationed in California.

After leaving the air force, he studied music at Ali Akbar College of Music in San Rafael, California, with tabla master Shankar Ghosh. Tabla is a type of Indian drum. Under the direction of Ghosh, Hart's interest in world music grew. He liked to listen to and study music from all parts of the globe. Listening to different types of music influenced Hart's playing.

Not long after the Grateful Dead was formed, Hart joined the group in 1967. He was twenty-four years old. He took what he learned from his tabla master back to rehearsals with Kreutzmann. Both had a keen interest in trying new forms of music. He and Bill Kreutzmann were nicknamed the Rhythm Devils. "They were known for their legendary drum solos—often lasting more than ten minutes," says McNally. "It was unusual for a rock band to have two drummers. But it worked because they both loved to improvise."[18]

Ron "Pigpen" McKernan

Ron "Pigpen" McKernan, born September 8, 1946, in San Bruno, California, was exposed to blues music at an early age. His father worked as a rhythm and blues disc jockey. The town of San Bruno also had a lot of blues music clubs. McKernan heard the music on the streets and in his home.

His parents encouraged his love of blues and other music. And like all of the members of the Grateful Dead, McKernan liked experimenting with music. He sang and played piano, percussion, guitar, and harmonica. He dropped out of high school to pursue a career in music. He officially began his musical career by playing piano in local bars.

While making the rounds at various California bars and coffeehouses, McKernan met Jerry Garcia. It was Garcia who nicknamed him Pigpen after the Peanuts character. Pigpen was a founding member of the Grateful Dead. He was their first keyboard player. His favorite form of music was the blues. It influenced his music, and he brought that sound to the group.

Between 1967 and 1968, Mickey Hart and newcomer keyboardist Tom Constanten pushed for a more psychedelic sound, driving out McKernan. He left the Dead, played on his own, and returned to the band in 1970.

During the early 1970s, the band experimented with drugs. McKernan's drug of choice was alcohol. Eventually, too much alcohol deteriorated his liver. He died at age twenty-seven on March 8, 1973, of a gastrointestinal hemorrhage.

Tom Constanten

Born March 19, 1944, in Long Branch, New Jersey, Tom Constanten joined the Grateful Dead in 1968 to supplement McKernan's organ playing.

Constanten met Phil Lesh in 1961 at UC Berkeley in California. He was studying astronomy. Constanten and Lesh became fast friends and roommates. He took music classes with Lesh. Both were students of Luciano Berio, who invited them to accompany him to Europe. Constanten jumped at the offer. Lesh stayed in California. While in Europe, Constanten studied with many notable contemporary classical musicians, including Pierre Boulez, Karlheinz Stockhausen, and Henri Pousseur. Upon his return to the States, he joined Lesh as a member of the Grateful Dead.

By 1970, he parted ways with the band and stayed in the Bay area throughout the 1970s, 1980s, and part of the 1990s. He taught piano, performed, and even composed music for the theater. In 1986, he became a resident artist at Harvard University.

Constanten was the only member of the band who didn't experiment with drugs. Instead, he followed Scientology, a New Age religion created by science-fiction writer L. Ron Hubbard.

Keith Godchaux

Born July 19, 1948, in San Francisco, California, Keith Godchaux always had music in his life. Keith's father was a professional pianist and singer. As a young child, Godchaux studied classical music. Although he loved classical music, he spent his teen years performing at country clubs in various jazz and rock and roll bands.

While performing in California coffeehouses and nightclubs, Godchaux met singer Donna Jean Thatcher. They got married in 1970.

Playing in various venues around California, Godchaux was drawn to the music of the Grateful Dead. He found out that they were looking for a keyboard player to replace McKernan. After a few months of performing with the Grateful Dead, he introduced his wife, Donna Jean, to the group. She was asked to join as a singer; they were Grateful Dead band members from October 1971 to February 1979.

Keith Godchaux was also part of the rock group New Riders of the Purple Sage. Godchaux's specialty was improvising jazz-influenced sounds, which he brought to the group. He also cowrote songs with Robert Hunter for the Grateful Dead and with Lowell George for the band Little Feat. Godchaux left the band in 1979. He died in an automobile accident in 1980 at age thirty-two.

Donna Jean Thatcher Godchaux MacKay

Donna Jean Thatcher was born August 22, 1947, in Sheffield, Alabama, where she was exposed to country and blues music. As a teenager, she started out as a session singer in Muscle Shoals, Alabama. When she got older, she moved to Memphis and Nashville. She worked as a backup singer for Elvis Presley, Aretha Franklin, and Otis Redding. In the late 1960s, she moved to the West Coast where she met her first husband, Keith Godchaux.

Donna and Keith Godchaux were part of the Grateful Dead from 1971 to 1979. She was the only woman in the group.

They also played in a band called Ghosts, which later became the Heart of Gold Band. In addition, they worked with Jerry Garcia on an album called *Keith and Donna*. Their son, Zion, was born in 1974.

In the mid-1970s, Donna Jean also toured with the Jerry Garcia Band, and the band Keith & Donna. A few years after her husband, Keith, died, she married Dave MacKay, a bass player, engineer, and music producer, who founded the group the Tazmanian Devils.

Brent Mydland

Brent Mydland was born on October 21, 1952, in Munich, Germany. His father served as a chaplain in the U.S. Army. When he was one year old, his father moved the family back to the States, settling in San Francisco. As a young child, Brent took piano lessons, studied classical music, and listened to jazz greats such as Herbie Hancock and Chick Correa. In high school, he formed his own rock band called Silver.

Brent Mydland was the fourth keyboardist for the Grateful Dead, replacing Keith Godchaux. He joined the Grateful Dead in 1979 after working on a solo project with Bob Weir and stayed on for eleven years. Throughout that time, he was referred to as "the new guy."

He loved being a part of the Grateful Dead. However, his life with the band had its ups and downs. The "ups" were the success of the band and playing the music he loved. The "downs" were being addicted to drugs. Shortly after completing a summer tour in 1990, he died of a drug overdose at age thirty-eight.

Vince Welnick

Born February 22, 1951, in Phoenix, Arizona, Vince Welnick studied piano and played keyboards as a young child. As a teenager, he formed his first rock band, the Beans. The Beans later became the Tubes when Welnick and fellow band members moved to San Francisco in 1969. The Tubes signed a record deal with A&M.

After the Tubes disbanded, Welnick heard that the Grateful Dead was looking for a replacement for Brent Mydland. He auditioned for the group and got hired. He was so nervous and shy at his first performance that he could barely play. Fortunately, the fans in the audience put him at ease. He was the keyboardist with the Grateful Dead from 1990 to 1995.

Welnick remained with the Grateful Dead until Jerry Garcia's death, when the group disbanded. After Garcia died, Welnick became severely depressed. He died at age fifty-five in 2006.

Bruce Hornsby

Born in 1954 in historic Williamsburg, Virginia, Bruce Hornsby was a part-time member of the Grateful Dead. He attended the University of Miami and the Berklee College of Music. After graduating, he and his brother John Hornsby performed in bars and sent demo tapes to record companies. In 1980, he and his brother moved to Los Angeles, where they spent three years writing music for 20th Century Fox. At 20th Century Fox, he met musician Huey Lewis. Bruce Hornsby produced and recorded material for Lewis. In 1985, Hornsby signed his band, the Range, to RCA.

Hornsby became a part-time member of the Grateful Dead from 1990 to 1992. He toured with the Dead in more than one hundred concerts in the United States and Europe. He was asked to join the band full-time, but his solo career was quite successful. A few of his solo hit songs include "The Way It Is," "Mandolin Rain," and "Every Little Kiss." He is a three-time Grammy winner who has sold more than 10 million records since his multi-platinum debut in 1986.

The Grateful Dead worked around his busy schedule. Hornsby appreciated the free-spirited nature of the band: "To be creative, spontaneous in the moment and make music in the present tense, that's what we're all about live. I write the songs, we make the records and then the records become a departure point, the basic blueprint, the basic arrangement. I'm fairly restless creatively. I was never a very good Top 40 band guy because I never liked to play the same thing every time. Too often songwriters approach their songs like museum pieces. I don't subscribe to that. I think of my songs as living beings that evolve and change and grow through the years."[19]

Hornsby also took delight with Grateful Dead fans. He referred to them as "adventurous music listeners."[20]

In the 1960s, the Grateful Dead lived on Ashbury Street in San Francisco, California. They lived, worked, and practiced together.

3

HISTORY OF THE BAND

In 1965, members of the Grateful Dead shared a communal home at 710 Ashbury Street in San Francisco. Thanks to the growing hippie movement in the Haight Ashbury neighborhood of San Francisco, communal living—or family-style living among friends—caught on. The members of the band lived, worked, and practiced together. "It was a relationship with disagreements and friendships," says Weir. "We worked, lived, and rehearsed together. When you are part of a band, you have to regard that band as your primary instrument. For me, my secondary instruments were my guitar and voice."[1]

They practiced often and built a large following thanks to the many free concerts in the San Francisco area in which they participated. The Grateful Dead was considered a leader of San Francisco's growing hippie movement.

In the mid-1960s, most people listened to AM radio stations. At the time, FM was a fairly new format. The Federal Communications Commission (FCC) ruled that FM stations had to play new material, not rehashes of the AM format. Many people listened to the local KMPX, which was a good start for the band.

To promote their music, Garcia, Lesh, and other band members called up radio stations asking to hear their own songs, thereby getting them played on the air. Garcia and Lesh discovered the fledgling KMPX station in San Francisco. KMPX was known as an "underground" (not mainstream) radio station. This fledgling radio station gave a lot of airtime to the Grateful Dead's music.

In 1966, they signed with MGM Records. Unfortunately, the recording sessions didn't go smoothly, so the record label dropped them. A short time later, in 1967, the Grateful Dead performed at the Fillmore Auditorium and other local venues to rave reviews. That same year, they signed with Warner Brothers and released their first album called *The Grateful Dead.*

Fans liked the album, but preferred watching them live. "We also preferred performing to studio recording," says Weir.

"The reaction from the audience was immediate and positive—which energized us."[2]

According to Weir, Lesh and all of the members of the band preferred playing before a live audience. Their second album, *Anthem of the Sun*, had a mix of live songs and recorded ones. In 1969, *Live Dead* was released. What made *Live Dead* such a success was that it was live—just as their fans preferred. The twenty-three-minute song "Dark Star" had incredible performances. It wasn't the type of music that fit into most radio formats. Songs on the radio often were between three and four minutes long. Still, the Grateful Dead were getting plenty of play on FM stations. They liked the improvisation, the jamming, lots of surprises, and just plain good music. At their concerts, songs could take different and longer formats.

"A studio record is a lot like building a ship in a bottle," Garcia once said, "whereas playing live is like being a rowboat on an ocean."[3]

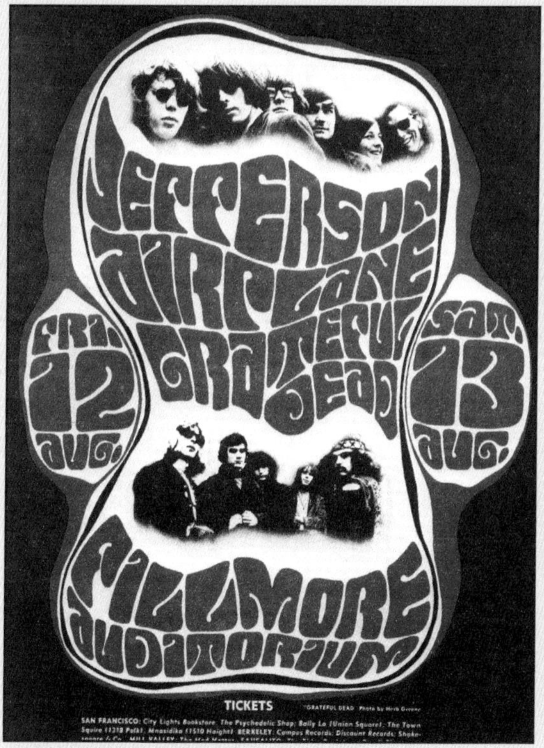

This concert poster advertised Jefferson Airplane and the Grateful Dead in concert at the Fillmore Auditorium in the 1960s.

In the mid-1970s, members of the band decided to make a movie. *The Grateful Dead* movie was billed as a concert experience. A *New York Times* critic wrote that the film didn't provide any personal details about the members of the band, which was fine for the fans. Robert Christgau, *Village Voice* movie critic, wrote in his June 13, 1977, review:

> The ignorant person who reviewed it for the *Times* complained that the film doesn't probe, which it certainly doesn't—it wouldn't be a Dead film if it did. What it does is lay out enough information for anyone who is genuinely curious to find out what the Dead are really about. The ticket hassles and awkward bodies, the spaced-out gibberish and inspired nonsense, the music with all its highs and lows—they're all here. In 50 years, when people want to know what a rock concert was like, they'll refer to this movie. But all they'll find out is what a Dead concert was like. It's not the same thing—not the same thing at all."[4]

Overall, the film was well received. Directed by Garcia and producer/director Leon Gast, it includes interviews with Jerry Garcia, Bob Weir, Phil Lesh, Mickey Hart, Bill Kreutzmann, Donna and Keith Godchaux, and their fans. The highlight is the concert footage, which comes from the five-night sold-out performance at San Francisco's Winterland in 1974. For fans, it is a pared down concert, which clocks in at two hours and twenty-one minutes, which they can replay over and over again.

4

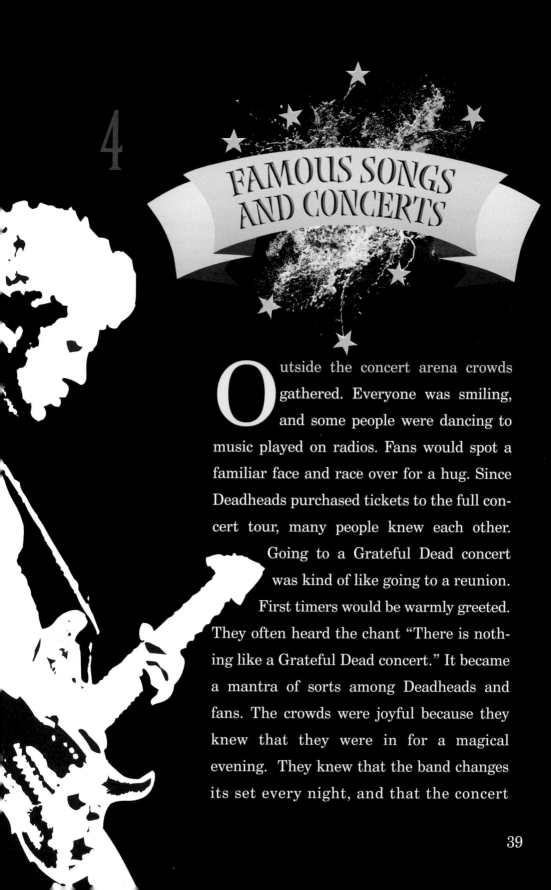

FAMOUS SONGS AND CONCERTS

Outside the concert arena crowds gathered. Everyone was smiling, and some people were dancing to music played on radios. Fans would spot a familiar face and race over for a hug. Since Deadheads purchased tickets to the full concert tour, many people knew each other.

Going to a Grateful Dead concert was kind of like going to a reunion. First timers would be warmly greeted. They often heard the chant "There is nothing like a Grateful Dead concert." It became a mantra of sorts among Deadheads and fans. The crowds were joyful because they knew that they were in for a magical evening. They knew that the band changes its set every night, and that the concert could run anywhere between two and four hours. For fans with tickets to every performance on the concert tour, they knew that each night's performance would introduce them to new songs, new versions of old favorites, and familiar tunes. They could tell if someone was off the mark or completely on game.

When members of the Grateful Dead walked onstage, everyone in the audience went wild. It didn't matter if it was at a large stadium like Madison Square Garden in New York City or a small concert hall like the Rainbow Theater in London, England. At a concert in 1981 at the Rainbow Theater, more than fifty people stood shoulder to shoulder. There were no seats in the small theater, and at 7:00 p.m. when the Grateful Dead walked in, the crowd quieted down. They just started playing and people started swaying to the music. People didn't call out during the performance like they do here in the States.

Back at the Meadowlands Arena in New Jersey, crowds started partying in the parking lot. Inside the stadium when a song was over, fans would call out the names of tunes they wanted the band to play. Even though this crowd was a bit loud, they still listened intently to the music, and many stood in front of their seats rocking from side to side. Some danced in the aisles.

The members of the Grateful Dead had a mission too. It was important for them to connect to the audience. Drummer Mickey Hart explains:

> There was nothing common among us except to enjoy. Jerry was kicked out of the Army, traveling, playing banjo. Bobby was from an upper class family, transferred among a number of high schools, and playing folk songs. Pigpen was good at playing blues harp and earned money for booze. Phil was a genius of classic violin and was into music theory and experimental music in college. Bill was playing in different R&B bands. And I mastered military drums and was dreaming of being a drummer in a big band jazz band. It was a miracle that all these guys coming from different places and musical background got together to form a band. Outcasts in respective worlds completed this strange puzzle just to enjoy ourselves.[1]

The audience felt that connection. For those who attended a hundred or more concerts, following a tour was a highlight. It never got boring because each member of the Grateful Dead pushed themselves musically. They liked improvising, which they couldn't do when they were recording albums, and stretching themselves to try new things. A concert could consist of American bluegrass, a little bit of country, rock, folk, and psychedelic songs.

If you went to a Dead concert in the 1970s and later in the 1980s, you were sure to hear a mixture of songs from different genres. Those who went to their first concert in the 1960s and stayed loyal to the end in the 1990s could easily tell if Jerry Garcia was well or not. The fans knew a lot about the band. They didn't swap personal stories about them. They talked about the music. It didn't matter if you came from Japan, England, Australia, or the States, it was the music that drew everyone together. Even teenagers who went to their first Grateful Dead concert in the 1980s went for the music. One nineteen year old remarked that she wasn't born when the Dead started touring. She said that she loved the concerts because of the music and the friendly crowds at each concert. Plus she could see that the band loved performing.

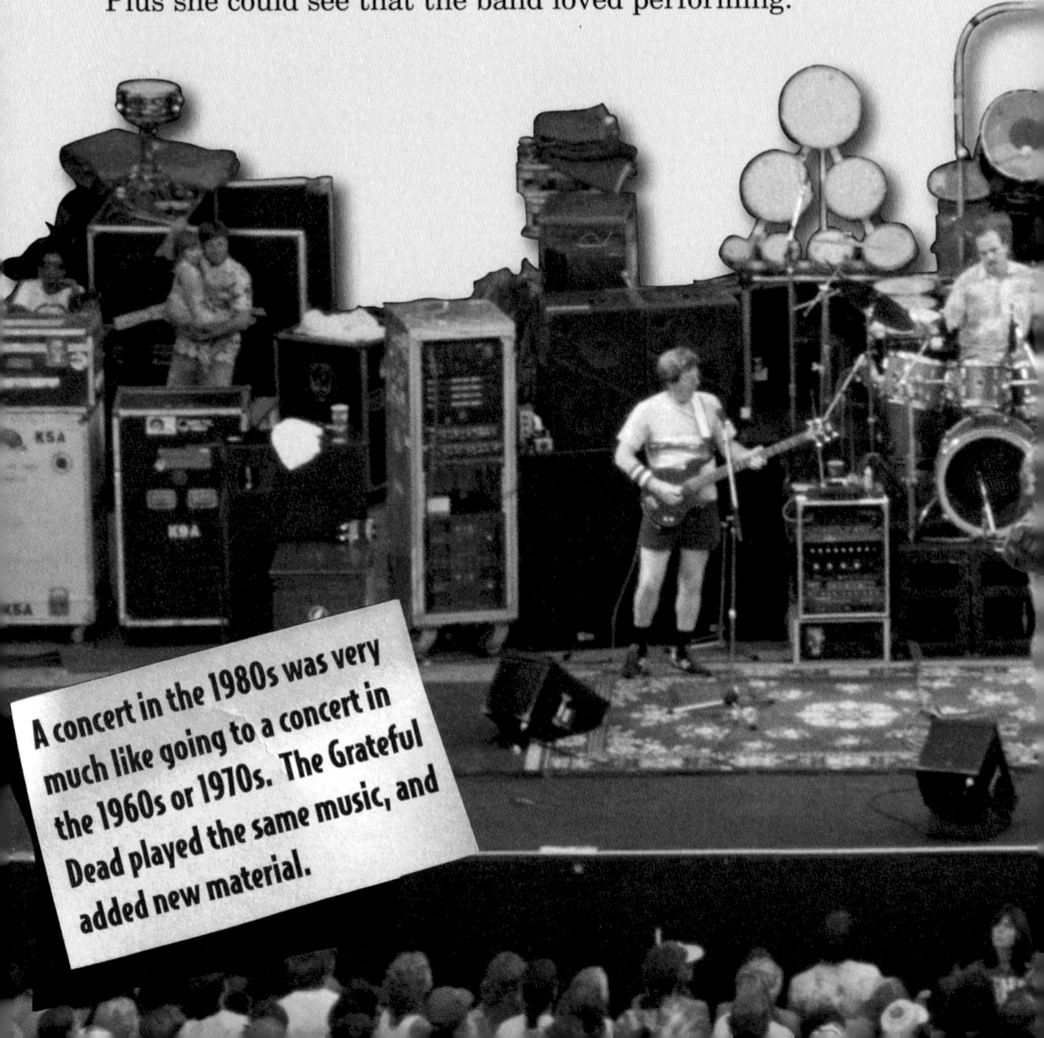

A concert in the 1980s was very much like going to a concert in the 1960s or 1970s. The Grateful Dead played the same music, and added new material.

The unity between the band and its audience was felt by everyone who attended a Grateful Dead concert. Their third live album, *Europe '72*, has the statement, "There is nothing like a Grateful Dead concert" in the liner notes. That sentiment rang true at all concerts and with their albums. They despised going into a recording studio to make an album. They preferred the connection with the audience, and improvising. "They didn't like being in the studio," says Dennis McNally. "It didn't suit them. Going to a concert was stunningly fun. It was about letting go of your regular consciousness."[2]

Many of their successful albums were recorded live. They also had several top-selling studio albums.

Their first song that was a hit was "Do You Believe in Magic?" by the Lovin' Spoonful. They also sang a lot of Bob Dylan songs. They had another hit on their hands with a song written by Memphis jug band player Noah Lewis. He wrote "Viola Lee."

Their career started taking off when Jerry Garcia and Robert Hunter collaborated on their own material. Their first big hit was "Dark Star," followed by "Saint Stephen" and "Sugar Magnolia."

"Their songs evolved slowly," says McNally. "By late 1967 and 1968, they became an experimental band. They were always changing styles and improvising. At that time, they wrote material for *Working Man's Dead*, which was a top-selling album. It has the song 'Uncle John's Band' in it, which is about the Grateful Dead."[3]

The album *American Beauty* followed *Working Man's Dead*. It was also a studio album that got rave reviews. Many of the songs in this album are also autobiographical of sorts, starting with "Truckin'," which is about life on the road.

One of the last studio albums they recorded, *In the Dark*, was released in 1987. It had one of the most loved Grateful Dead songs, "A Touch of Grey." When you hear this song at a concert and they sing the chorus declaring that they "will get by," fans shout their approval. They know that the Dead and everyone in the concert hall have battled highs and lows. In the Grateful Dead's case, those ups and downs included drug and alcohol addiction, death of band members, illness, and breakups of personal relationships. The line stating that they "will get by" boosts everyone's confidence; it really speaks to everyone who is familiar with the music because the Grateful Dead's philosophy is that we all face adversity. It doesn't matter. It's just life, and while we are here we should do our best to enjoy life.

A crowd dances at a Grateful Dead concert in the 1970s.

5

DEADHEADS

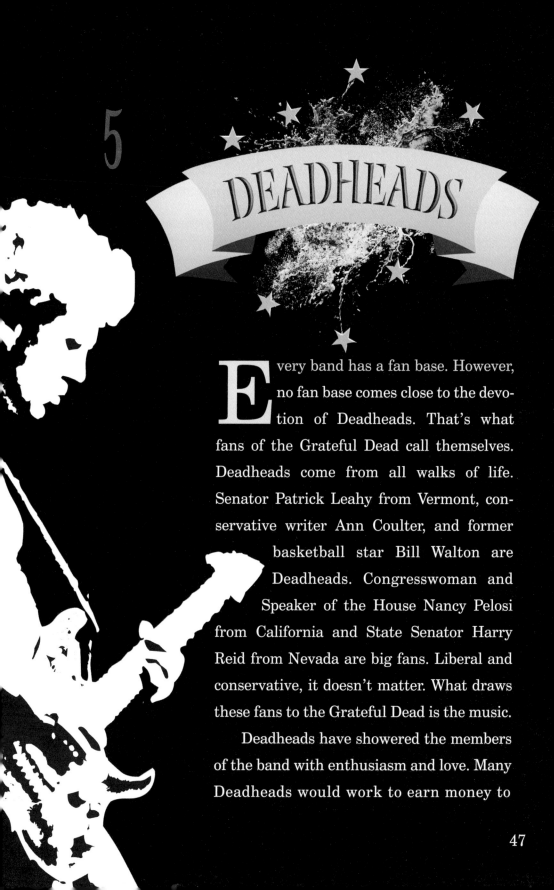

Every band has a fan base. However, no fan base comes close to the devotion of Deadheads. That's what fans of the Grateful Dead call themselves. Deadheads come from all walks of life. Senator Patrick Leahy from Vermont, conservative writer Ann Coulter, and former basketball star Bill Walton are Deadheads. Congresswoman and Speaker of the House Nancy Pelosi from California and State Senator Harry Reid from Nevada are big fans. Liberal and conservative, it doesn't matter. What draws these fans to the Grateful Dead is the music.

Deadheads have showered the members of the band with enthusiasm and love. Many Deadheads would work to earn money to attend a series of Grateful Dead concerts. Once they had their money in hand, they would purchase as many concert tickets as possible, quit their jobs, and go on the road to see as many concerts as they possibly could afford. When the Grateful Dead weren't performing, most Deadheads worked. "So many of us would work with the goal of seeing the Grateful Dead—that was our reward," says Jane Healy.[1]

The sheer numbers of Deadheads are mind-blowing. Deadheads are on every continent of the globe; they still listen to the music. They enjoy reminiscing about past concerts and look forward to attending new ones by former members of the Grateful Dead.

"It's a reunion of sorts when you go to a Ratdog, Phil Lesh and Friends, or Mickey Hart concert," says Healy. "I just went to see Bob Weir of Ratdog perform at New York's Beacon Theater, and I saw so many familiar faces from long ago. It's a good feeling to reconnect with other Deadheads."[2]

The music of the offshoot bands is different, but the spirit is the same. For Deadheads, the members of the Grateful Dead really gave and still give their all in concert. "What I liked best was the element of surprise," says Healy. "At Grateful Dead concerts, fans would be treated to new versions of old favorites, and often members of the Grateful Dead didn't come onstage with a playlist. They knew that many of the fans in the audience saw the concert the night before and will probably see it again tomorrow. So, they would even perform different versions of the same songs."[3]

For members of the Grateful Dead, "the music happened between the stage and the audience," says Bob Weir. He further explains: "The two met in the air somewhere. We would come on and play. We really could tune into each others' thoughts and knew what we were going to play. We did discuss the first few songs that we were going to play, but after that we would wing it. We liked jamming and performing different versions of the same songs. We wanted to have a good time, and we wanted our audience to have a good time too."[4]

Deadheads would travel the country following the band. "Where the Grateful Dead went, we went," says John Ganrahan, better known as Cub. He got that name for being good with maps—like a Cub Scout. "My friends and I are based on the East Coast. So we would go up and down the East Coast to attend several Grateful Dead concerts. I always had a map and never got lost. I was good at navigating."[5]

Cub admits to violating the rules of how many people were allowed in the rooms of the local motels and sacrificing comfort for the chance to see his favorite band:

> Sometimes there were twelve of us. The accommodations weren't important. We wanted to see the shows. We would drive across the country from our homes in New Jersey to follow the Dead. We mainly traveled up and down the East Coast. Occasionally, we would travel to California or Colorado. The concerts on the West Coast

> were much more mellow than those on the East Coast. Here, the pace was faster. And every performance was different—even during the same tour. The Dead knew that their fans often purchased sets of tickets. So, they would play different songs at each concert. Every concert was a totally different experience from the previous ones. Sometimes they would perform a new take on a standard tune. Seeing them in person was just amazing.[6]

Cub wasn't alone in his quest to see as many Grateful Dead shows as possible. "It was a great time," he says. "So many friendships formed. We met so many good people along the way. Even if we had differences, the music brought us together."[7]

Cub took a variety of jobs when the Grateful Dead were not on tour. He pumped gas and designed kitchens. The work was temporary and enabled him to make enough money to go on the road to hear the music. Other Deadheads took temporary jobs in order to follow the band on tour. Jane Healy excelled at cooking. She would sell food right before the concerts. She usually traveled with a small grill to barbecue food outside the arenas where the Grateful Dead were performing. She explains: "I would scope out the area and check out the local markets. Then I would purchase food to cook outside the concert halls about an hour or two before a Dead concert. I sold a lot of food and the money I made enabled me to purchase more tickets. I mostly saw their East Coast concerts, but on occasion, I would travel all over the globe to listen to their music. Cooking was a good way to make money for hotel rooms, gas for the car, and of course Grateful Dead tickets."[8]

Healy was eighteen when she left home and went to her first Grateful Dead concert. "I went with a few friends and we would share the cost of gas, food, and hotel rooms," she says. "My parents weren't too wild about me being on the road, but it was a different time then. I traveled with my friends. We always stayed in a group and it felt safe. I was so drawn to their [Grateful Dead's] music that the travel was so worth it to me."[9]

Cub fully understands. He first heard of the Grateful Dead through his sister Katie. "She went to her first show in 1978," he says. "I listened to the music on the radio, and instantly liked it. It was a mix of music—one that you couldn't put into a category. I guess I liked that. It was magic seeing them perform, and definitely worth working odd jobs to be able to attend the concerts."[10]

Cub's home is filled with homemade tapes from various Grateful Dead concerts. He explains:

> I was a taper. The Grateful Dead allowed their fans to tape their concerts. Actually, they set up an area near the stage for people who wanted to tape the concerts. It was exciting because we were so close to the stage. We really felt special walking past the crowds to our space near the stage that was just for us—a place where we could listen and tape these concerts. It's a bit of history.

> We also had an honor code. We didn't sell the tapes. Taping a concert allowed us to come home with an incredible memory that we could play over and over again. We could trade tapes, but never make any money by selling them.[11]

Cub didn't get mixed up in drugs. "I couldn't," he notes. "I took taping seriously. Taping and drugs just didn't mix. I am lucky because I have a large collection of music from their concerts."[12]

TAPE RECORDING A CONCERT WAS ALLOWED AND ACCEPTED AT GRATEFUL DEAD CONCERTS. THERE WERE SPECIAL SECTIONS IN THE AUDIENCE FOR "TAPERS."

There are many fond memories. Cub says, "For me, I loved watching Jerry [Garcia] play. His style of playing and the way he played—even with one part of a finger missing—was incredible. He would play with a pick and hold the pick with his stub. In the middle of a song he would stop playing with the pick, use the stub to hold the pick and play with his fingernails to get a totally different sound. Then he would go back to playing with the pick again. It happened so fast and seemed like it came so easy to him.[13]

Although all members of the band were of equal importance, Cub admits he favored Jerry Garcia. "Jerry didn't want to be the star of the band, but to me, he was. A lot of the girls liked Bob Weir. Everyone had their favorites. For me, when I was at a show and he looked at you and smiled, you got energized."[14]

Megan McWilliams understood that feeling. As a teenager in the 1970s, she sat high up on a friend's shoulders staring eye to eye with Bob Weir. "I know that every girl thought he was singing to them," she says. "During the song 'Sugar Magnolia,' I swear he smiled at me. I was fifteen or sixteen at the time."[15]

McWilliams was seven years old when she first heard the Grateful Dead. "I was singing along to a Dead song that was playing on the radio in my sister's pickup truck," she says. "My brother and sister are eight and ten years older than me.

They took me with them to Dead concerts. I know every note of every song."[16]

"What drew me to the Dead was that you couldn't categorize their music," McWilliams says. "They started out playing folk and bluegrass music, later switched to their version of psychedelic and rock, and moved back to bluegrass and folk. It was a combination of all forms of music, and it worked."[17]

Despite a mixture of sounds, the Dead could be heard on AM and FM radio stations throughout the country in the late 1960s, 1970s, 1980s, and 1990s. In the 1970s, a handful of their songs were censored. Their songs had words that may seem tame by today's standards.

Justin Ben-Asher, a student at Yale University, listened to the Grateful Dead's music growing up. His parents were fans, who played—and still play—the music they grew up with. Ben-Asher describes himself as a fan who started a radio show at Yale "to share the music I love with my peers."[18]

His radio show at Yale was called *Rock and Rye*. He explains, "The name comes from a line in a Grateful Dead song 'Mississippi Half-Step Uptown Toodeloo.' It refers literally to an old whiskey drink, but has added significance in that, well, rock you can figure out; and rye mold is used in producing LSD."[19] Ben-Asher continues: "I started the show during my junior year and modeled it loosely on David Gans's nationally syndicated Grateful Dead Hour radio program. [David Gans is a musician whose Grateful Dead Hour can be heard on several stations throughout the country.] I typically played selections from a single performance every week—usually a Grateful Dead performance, something from the Jerry Garcia Band or Garcia and Grisman."[20] David Grisman is a bluegrass and jazz musician who teamed up with Jerry Garcia on a few record albums.

The nationally syndicated Grateful Dead Hour draws fans from all over the country. "We get listeners of all ages—from older folks to younger people who found it for the first time," says David Gans. "We get a lot of feedback from our listeners. Many of them were not old enough to see them live. They found the radio show by accident or someone turns them on to it."[21]

"There are bigger bands than the Grateful Dead," admits Gans, but he continues, "What attracted so many people to their music is that the music is very deep and rich, fully telling and left a lot of room for interpretation. [Robert] Hunter's songs don't cough up meaning.

Deadheads still enjoy the music even today.

Each time you listen, you get a new perspective. These songs keep continuing to reward the listener. They are not filled with cheap sentiments about teenage mating rituals. The Grateful Dead's music is engaging, and it filled so many categories. It is much more than a rock and roll band."[22]

The members of the Grateful Dead learned a thing or two from Deadheads. "There was always so much encouragement, to just really take it and run with it, from Deadheads," says Lesh.[23] And that's what they did.

6

THE WORLD AROUND THEM: 1960s–1990s

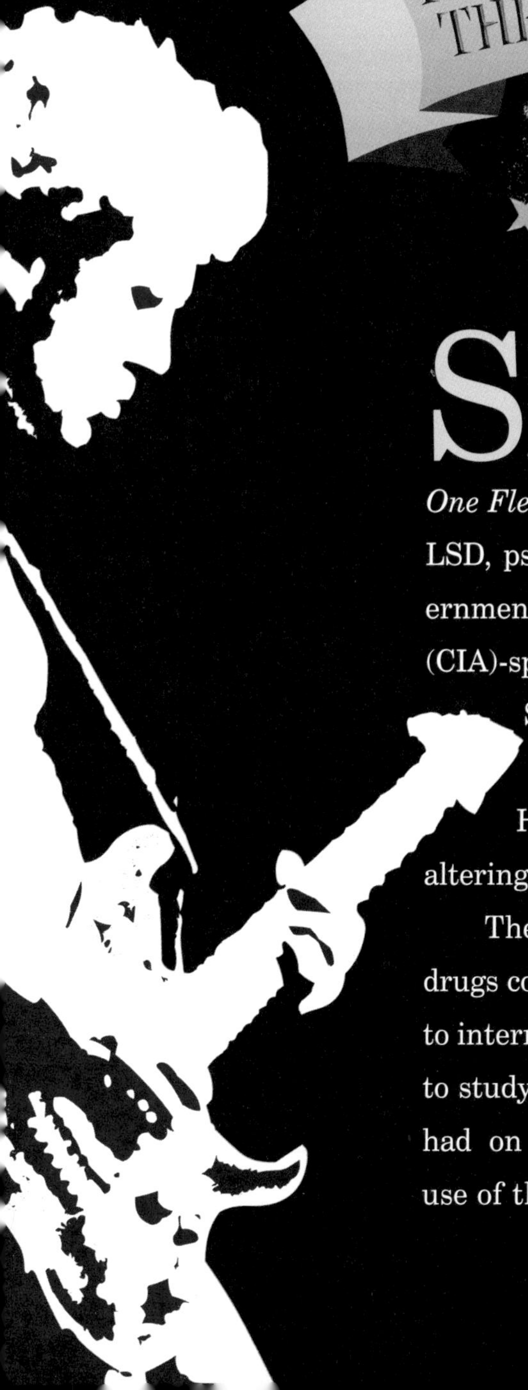

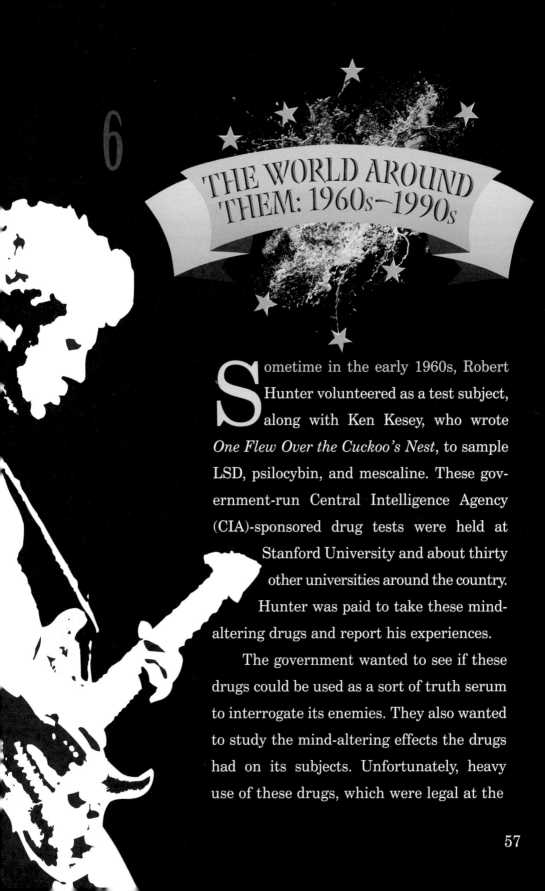

Sometime in the early 1960s, Robert Hunter volunteered as a test subject, along with Ken Kesey, who wrote *One Flew Over the Cuckoo's Nest*, to sample LSD, psilocybin, and mescaline. These government-run Central Intelligence Agency (CIA)-sponsored drug tests were held at Stanford University and about thirty other universities around the country. Hunter was paid to take these mind-altering drugs and report his experiences.

The government wanted to see if these drugs could be used as a sort of truth serum to interrogate its enemies. They also wanted to study the mind-altering effects the drugs had on its subjects. Unfortunately, heavy use of these drugs, which were legal at the time, took a toll on the public and the members of the band. Vince Welnick, a keyboardist with the Dead, died from a drug overdose. Brent Mydland, the fourth keyboardist with the Dead, also died of a drug overdose. At the time many rock bands experimented with drugs. For members of the Grateful Dead, psychedelic drugs were tools to create a different musical sound.

In the early years of the 1960s, the harmful effects of drugs were not well-known. LSD and other drugs often flowed freely at rock concerts. Music and drugs coexisted. Those band members who experimented with drugs often created a new sound called psychedelic music. Psychedelic music is music that is inspired by mind-altering experiences. The Grateful Dead practically invented this musical genre.

The Haight Ashbury section of San Francisco, where the Grateful Dead lived, was the center of this cultural scene. The expression "make love not war" started here and moved across the country and into Europe and other countries. Haight Ashbury was also the place where crowds of young people, called hippies, gathered to experiment with LSD and other mind-altering drugs. Hippies were opposed to establishment, against the Vietnam War, and wanted to live in a free society that believed in sharing ideas, questioning rules, and helping one another. They expressed their ideas through dance, art, and music.

THE 1960s WERE A TIME OF PROTEST. THIS YOUNG WOMAN HANDS A FLOWER AS A SIGN OF PEACE TO MILITARY POLICE.

Members of the Grateful Dead expressed their ideas through their music. “They didn’t write antiwar or protest songs,” says publicist Dennis McNally. “Music was an escape for the Dead and their fans. It was a way to express joy. They respected people’s opinions and didn’t want to sound preachy. Plus, they all were exposed to different forms of music at early stages in their lives. Their music is a rich mix of different musical genres.”[1]

The time was ripe for the Grateful Dead. They were truly at the right place at the right time when they formed in the mid-1960s. The Grateful Dead members were musical leaders with their counterculture music.

"We came out of that whole Beatnik [a hippie] ethos, you know, where success was really besides the point," says Garcia. "How well we play together was always more important than the money. That attitude, I think is partly the reason why things have gone the way they have."[2]

For hippies, the 1960s weren't about making money. It was a time of freedom, a movement away from the conservative values of the 1950s. Artists such as Alexander Calder wanted people to see playful images in his sculptures. Andy Warhol transformed ordinary household objects into art forms. Even Jerry Garcia created modern drawings and paintings reflecting his music and observations. He worked in pen and ink, acrylics, watercolors, and digital media.

Books reflected the era as well. Members of the Grateful Dead were fans of Beat writers and poets Jack Kerouac, Allen Ginsberg, Ken Kesey, and William Burroughs. (Beat writers rejected conventional social values.) The unconventional styles of Jack Kerouac influenced Garcia and other members of the Grateful Dead.

Many of the radical movements that began in the 1960s continued to gain momentum in the 1970s. People grew more disillusioned with the Vietnam War and the way the government ran the nation. The Watergate proceedings led to the resignations of Vice President Spiro Agnew and President Richard Nixon. Both were close to being impeached. The women's movement and the civil rights movement took a deeper hold. The culture was changing and the hippie movement was still going strong through the mid-1970s.

In the late 1970s, making money started to matter. Most of the members of the Dead had families to support. Members of the Grateful Dead took artistic control over their contracts and products. "We had a good deal at Warner Brothers," Garcia told Billboard magazine writer Dick Nesser. "Basically what we did was tear up the standard contract and write our own. We weren't stupid, you know. We had a lot of experience on the street, hustling deals, working bars. We entered the business at the time it was taking a 360-degree economic turn."[3]

The members of the Dead changed the wording on their contracts—the part of the contracts that affected their royalties. Royalties are the fees that are paid to performers. Garcia told Nesser, "Basically, you got paid for each cut, but some of our cuts were very long so we would've been cheated. Standard songs that played on the radio average about three minutes long. Our contract called for us to be paid for every three-minute interval of music on the album."[4]

Not too long after signing with Warner Brothers, the Grateful Dead wanted more control over their records. So in

1970, they formed their own record label called Ice Nine. The name Ice Nine comes from Kurt Vonnegut's book *Cat's Cradle*. In Vonnegut's novel, Ice Nine is a room that contains headaches. To the members of the Grateful Dead, dealing with record contracts was a headache.

Musically, the 1980s were a tough time for the Dead—mostly because of Garcia's heroin addiction, which he was constantly battling. In 1981, the Grateful Dead came out with *Dead Set*, a live album, and had a six-year hiatus from recording. They kept on touring to sold-out shows. Fans would introduce the music to their friends, siblings, and children. Younger generations of fans were formed.

Throughout the years, Garcia had to watch his diet and health. He went into a diabetic coma in 1986 and was close to death. He tried taking better care of himself. In 1987, the Dead released the album *In the Dark*. The album contained the song

In 1987, Bob Dylan (center) took the stage with Grateful Dead.

at was followed by the album *Built to Last*, which came t to poor reviews in 1989. *Built to Last* was their last dio album.

The Dead also experienced hardships during the1990s. In 92, Garcia was hospitalized with diabetes and an enlarged art. They had to cancel upcoming tours. Because of Garcia's health, the band toured less and less. On August 5, 1995, rcia checked himself into Serenity Knolls, a drug treatment nter in Marin County, California. Four days later, on August he died of a fatal heart attack.

The reaction to his death was overwhelming. Within a v hours of his death, more than one hundred thousand post-gs were made on the Internet. An all-night vigil was held in n Francisco, and the mayor called for all flags to be flown at lf-mast.

Jerry Garcia's death meant the end of the Grateful Dead. e members just didn't want to continue without their se friend.

Jerry Garcia was a beloved member of the Grateful Dead

7

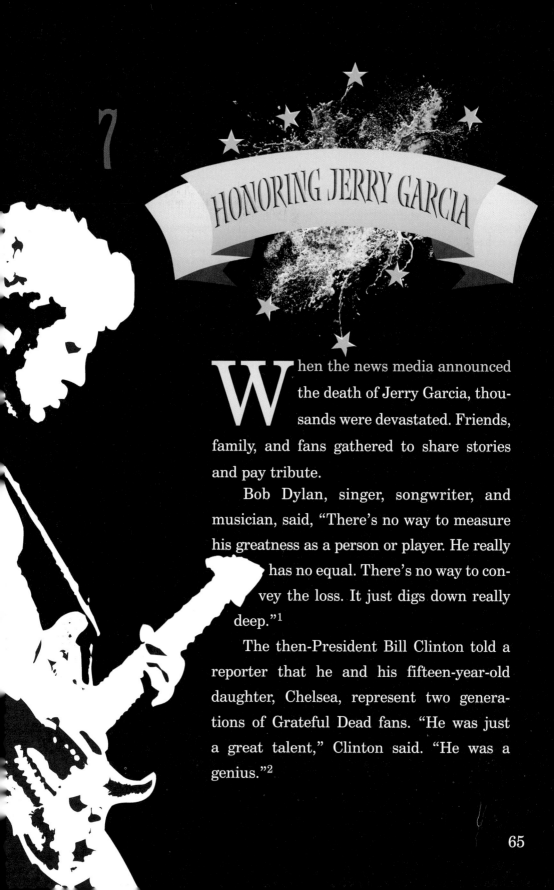

HONORING JERRY GARCIA

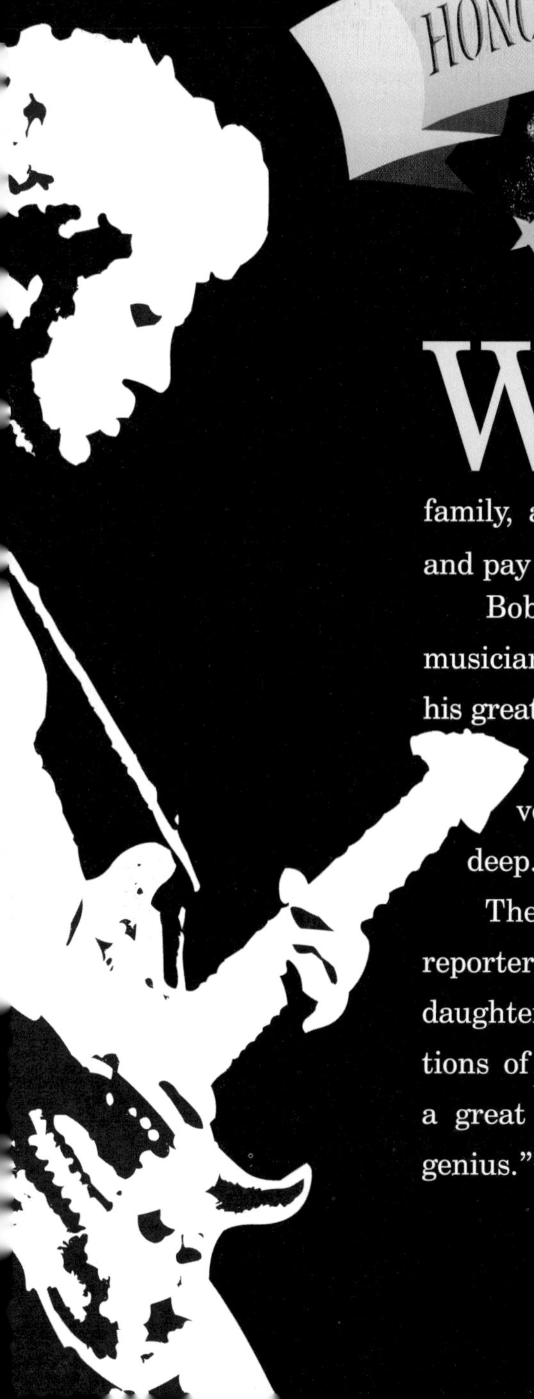

When the news media announced the death of Jerry Garcia, thousands were devastated. Friends, family, and fans gathered to share stories and pay tribute.

Bob Dylan, singer, songwriter, and musician, said, "There's no way to measure his greatness as a person or player. He really has no equal. There's no way to convey the loss. It just digs down really deep."[1]

The then-President Bill Clinton told a reporter that he and his fifteen-year-old daughter, Chelsea, represent two generations of Grateful Dead fans. "He was just a great talent," Clinton said. "He was a genius."[2]

This is a memorial to Jerry Garcia at the Polo Fields in San Francisco, California, a few days after Garcia's death.

Fans throughout the world felt his absence. "When I got the news of his death, I was on a job site in Atlanta," says Cub. "I mail ordered tickets to an upcoming concert, and the news just broke. I was devastated. It took me a long time to get over his death. It was a blow to the community. Deadheads are a community of close friends—like a family."[3]

Cub and other fans reminisced about Garcia and the Grateful Dead. "Jerry would do solo tours in between Grateful

Dead concerts," says Cub. "He had his own repertoire. His death was a great loss to his fans, to the music industry, and to the world. Personally, I fell into a deep depression. It was a sad time. It was like losing a good friend."[4]

Leading rock bands have their following, but the Grateful Dead had an impact on the world around them. The Grateful Dead produced thirty-one albums in twenty-eight years. Songs like "Truckin'," "Alabama Getaway," "Casey Jones," and "Sugar Magnolia" are just a few that fell into the mainstream in the United States and abroad.

In the 1980s, Garcia's artwork could be found on shirts, eyewear, and ties—even though Garcia never wore a tie. A leading ice cream manufacturer called Ben & Jerry's named a flavor after Garcia. "Cherry Garcia" is a mix of vanilla ice cream with bing cherries and thick flakes of chocolate. It is one of the most popular flavors on the market. The Republic of Tea, a leading manufacturer of tea, created "Jerry Cherry," a cherry-and-vanilla-flavored tea. Clos du Bois Winery in Sonoma County partnered with the Garcia estate to produce a series of limited edition bottles of wine; the labels feature his art. Deadheads also petitioned for a Jerry Garcia stamp. "We think it's a great petition," says McNally. "And as usual, it was the Deadheads themselves who started it. It wasn't us."[5]

Jerry Garcia is in the Rock and Roll Hall of Fame and on the Walk of Fame outside San Francisco's Bill Graham Civic Auditorium. In the Excelsior neighborhood of San Francisco, where Garcia grew up, an amphitheater in McLaren Park is named in his honor.

Following his death, Garcia's wife, Deborah Koons Garcia, and Bob Weir sprinkled his ashes down the Ganges River, 155 miles north of New Delhi in India on April 4. A ceremony followed with Koons Garcia and Weir immersing themselves in the Ganges.

When they returned to San Francisco, Garcia's remaining ashes were scattered in the San Francisco Bay on the morning of April 15, 1996. On that day, close friends and family gathered to hear poems written by Mickey Hart and Robert Hunter. Garcia is survived by his third wife, Deborah Koons Garcia, and four daughters—Heather, Annabelle, Teresa, and Keelin.

"The band fell apart when Jerry Garcia died," says McNally. "He was deeply loved—flaws and all. And those flaws made him Jerry. He wasn't supposed to be a guru or a teacher."[6]

Although many of his fans did think of him in those terms, he tried to let his fans know that he was an ordinary man who loved music. In an interview he did with Mary Eisenhart of *BAM Magazine* in 1995, he said:

> You know yourself for the person who makes mistakes, and that's capable of being *really stupid*, and doing stupid things. I don't know who you'd have to be to believe that kind of stuff about yourself, to believe that you were

somehow special. If I start believing that kind of stuff, everybody's going to just turn around and walk away from me. Nobody would let me get away with it, not for a minute. That's the strength of having a group. For me it's easier to believe a group than it is a person. Certainly one of the things that make the Grateful Dead interesting, from my point of view, is that it's a *group* of people. The dynamics of the group is the part that I trust.[7]

ART, IN ALL FORMS, WAS IMPORTANT TO JERRY GARCIA. THESE OIL PAINTINGS BY JERRY GARCIA WERE ON DISPLAY IN 2006 AT A GALLERY IN SAN FRANCISCO.

In an earlier interview with Eisenhart in 1987, he said, "Remember who we are? We are in reality a group of misfits, crazy people, who have voluntarily come together to work this stuff out and do the best we can, and try to be as fair as we possibly can with each other."[8]

Jerry Garcia and the Grateful Dead influenced a lot of musicians—particularly a band called Phish. Phish, like the Dead, preferred live performances. Many fans and music critics compare the two bands. In a 1999 interview with the *New York Post*, Trey Anastasio, lead singer and songwriter for Phish, said, "We are not the same band. It must be said they were and remain one of my favorite bands. In fact, the Dead are one of the most important American bands, if not the most important. To me, the Dead are a genuine link to traditional American music. They moved music history forward. Jerry Garcia was as important a figure in this country's music history as Bill Monroe or Elvis. Phish has learned a lot from them. They are an influence. The most important lesson we learned from the Dead was how to be a live band."[9]

Other tributes were held in Garcia's honor. On September 24, 2005, at the Greek Theater in Berkeley, California, surviving members of the Grateful Dead, the Jerry Garcia Band, Ratdog, performer Bruce Hornsby, and members of Phish performed Grateful Dead songs. Fans came out for a heartfelt tribute.

The music continues today. Members of the band keep in touch and will occasionally perform together. When they do get together, they play new songs and Grateful Dead songs. Musician Bruce Hornsby told a radio host on National Public Radio that when he performs today, he still gets requests from his audience to play Grateful Dead tunes.

For Garcia, it was all about the music. "You do not merely want to be considered just the best of the best," he said. "You want to be considered the only ones who do what you do."[10] According to fellow musicians and their fans, the Grateful Dead did just that—they were unique.

8

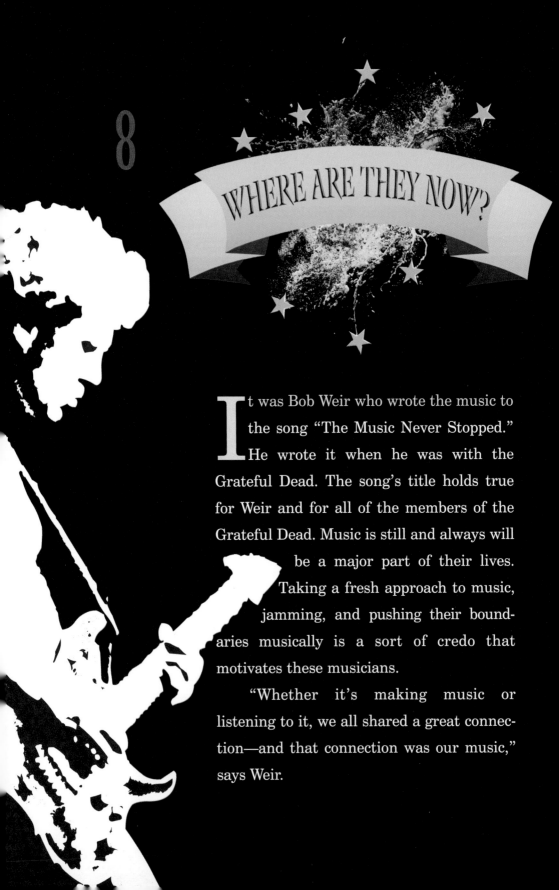

WHERE ARE THEY NOW?

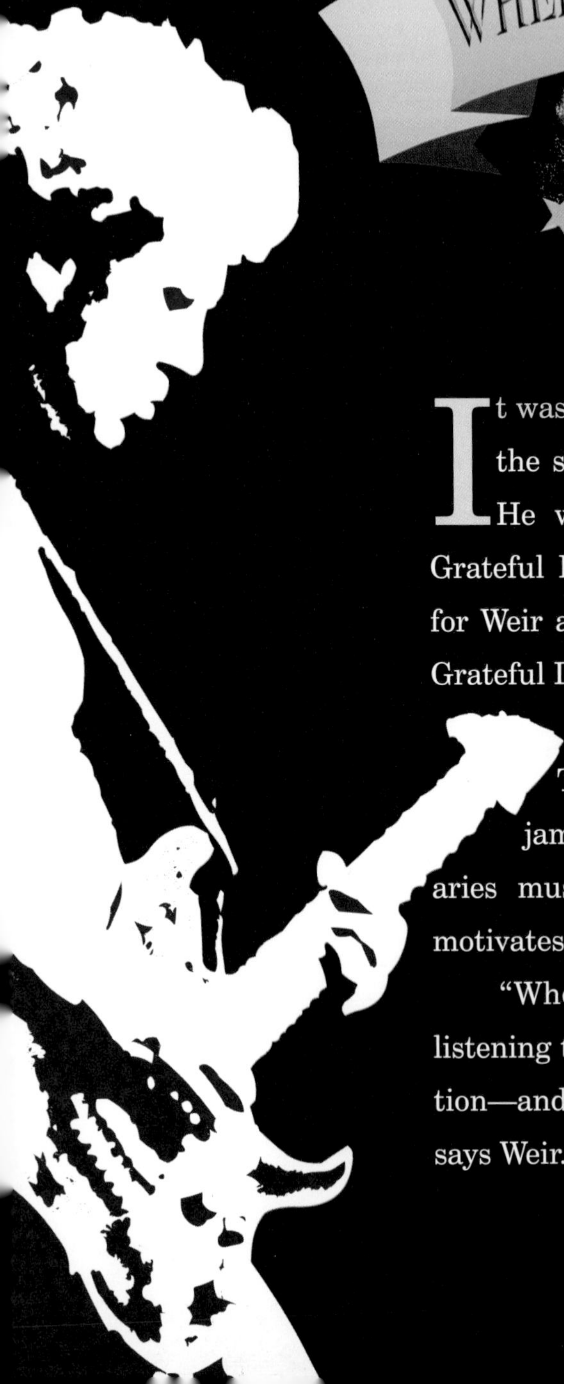

It was Bob Weir who wrote the music to the song "The Music Never Stopped." He wrote it when he was with the Grateful Dead. The song's title holds true for Weir and for all of the members of the Grateful Dead. Music is still and always will be a major part of their lives. Taking a fresh approach to music, jamming, and pushing their boundaries musically is a sort of credo that motivates these musicians.

"Whether it's making music or listening to it, we all shared a great connection—and that connection was our music," says Weir.

> It's special what we had, and it's special playing with other great musicians. Each musician we played with brings their own style to the mix. As a musician and a person who loves listening to music, I love variety—all of us did. That variety often turns up in our music. We learned by playing with one another and by listening to great music. We found sounds that inspired and excited us. I found that the music you love the most will have the most spirit to it. None of us tried to emulate trends in music. We just did what felt best with the Grateful Dead and with our own bands.[1]

Today, Bob Weir, Phil Lesh, Mickey Hart, Bill Kreutzmann, Robert Hunter, Tom Constanten, and Donna Jean Godchaux-MacKay continue to make music. A few of the members have formed their own bands. Others write and perform solo.

Bob Weir

While with the Grateful Dead, Weir formed a side band called Kingfish in 1976. In 1981, he created Bobby and the Midnites. He later hooked up with bassist Rob Wasserman and the duo Weir and Wasserman were born. Over the next few years, Weir and Wasserman would perform together and add new players to their band. In the late 1990s, Ratdog was formed. Wasserman left Ratdog in 2003 to pursue other projects. Still, Weir and Wasserman remain friends and occasionally perform together.

For Weir and the other former Grateful Dead members, the music they started their careers with will always be a part of their futures. "We like mixing sounds—whether it's bluegrass, psychedelic rock, or blues, we like to experiment with music," says Weir. "I did that with the Grateful Dead, and I'm doing that now with Ratdog."[2]

The formula seems to be working for Weir and the other members of the Grateful Dead. Ratdog's first album, *Evening Moods*, was released in 2000 to favorable reviews. Ratdog's second album, *Ratdog Live at Roseland*, was

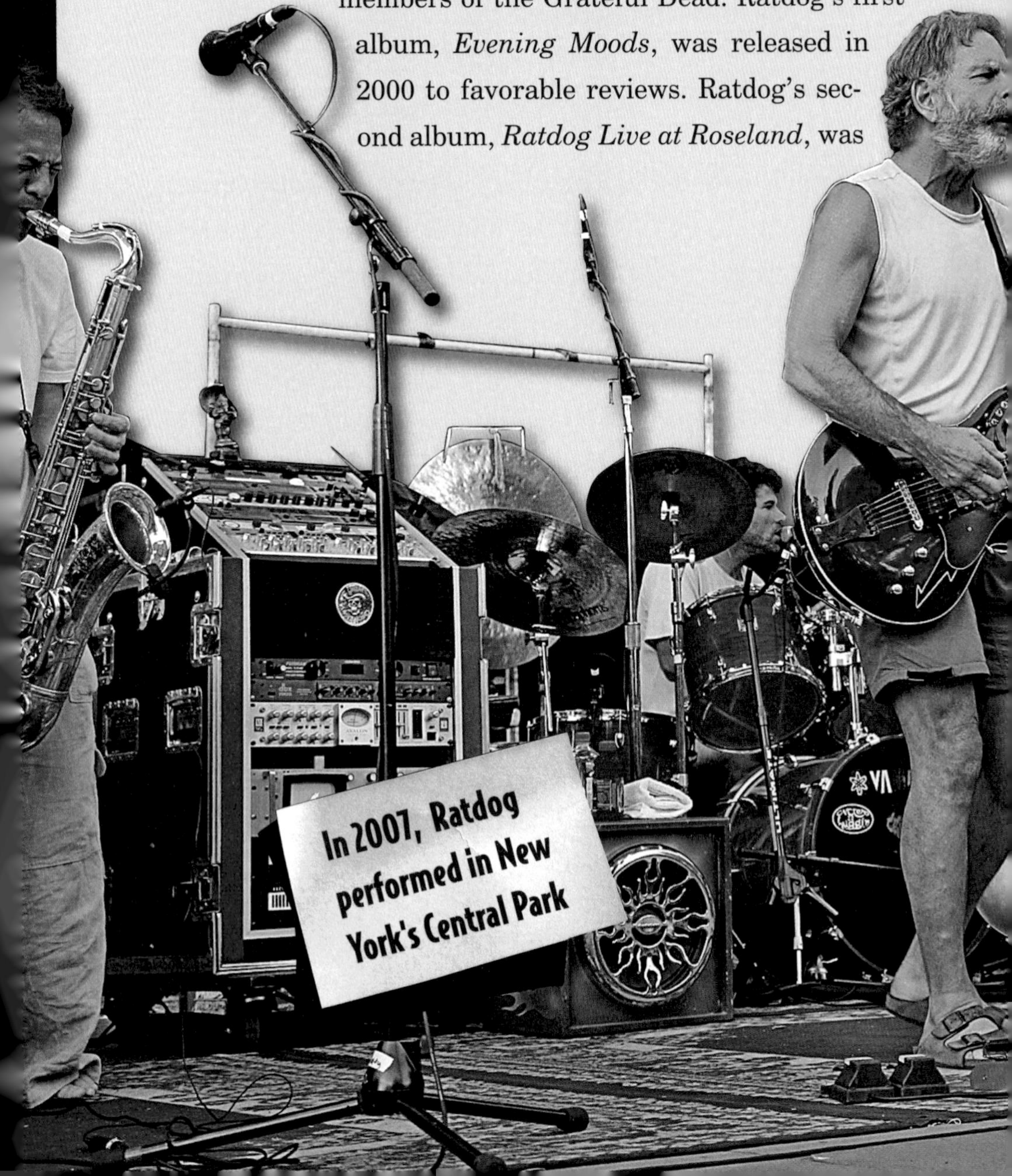

In 2007, Ratdog performed in New York's Central Park

a double CD collection from a Portland, Oregon, show. This 2001-released CD was a big hit with Deadheads. Some of the newer members in the audience refer to themselves as Dogheads. Like Deadheads, Dogheads prefer live albums to studio-recorded versions. So Weir has continued a Grateful Dead tradition of recording live concerts into albums.

When Weir isn't performing, he spends time with his family in California. Weir is married and has two daughters. He is also close to his sister, Wendy Weir. They coauthored a children's book titled *Panther Dream: A Story of the African Rainforest*. Weir also wrote and his sister illustrated the children's book *Baru Bay Australia*.

“I like writing, but it's the music that drives me,” he explains. “All I foresee is writing, recording, and touring.”[3]

When he is at home, his family listens to a wide range of music. “I'm a big proponent of music education,” he says. “My older daughter is taking violin lessons. My five year old bangs on the piano. I don't push them. They have music around them and they seem to take to it positively. My older daughter is singing and recording a song in the living room right now. I let them follow their own dreams.”[4]

Phil Lesh

Fans of the wiry-thin bassist Phil Lesh had a nickname for the spot onstage where Lesh performed with the Grateful Dead. It was known as the Phil Zone. Here is where Lesh powered his electric bass guitar to the delight of his followers. Today Lesh performs in the band Phil Lesh and Friends. He formed his band shortly after Jerry Garcia died. The lineup of “Friends” in the band changes from concert tour to concert tour. Sometimes the “Friends” can include members from the Grateful Dead. Phil Lesh and Friends spend a great deal of time on the road.

Unfortunately, in 1991, Lesh was diagnosed with hepatitis C. He believes he got infected sometime in the mid-1960s. In 1998, his doctor told him he had prostrate cancer. Lesh underwent surgery in December 1998. The surgery was a success, and he credits part of his recovery to Grateful Dead fans.

The Sunday before his surgery, Deadheads across the globe held a five-minute worldwide prayer. Lesh believes that the prayers helped him toward a speedy recovery.

The following year, he was on the road again performing with his band. He also produced a live solo album called *Love Will See You Through*. After the release of his album to positive reviews, he went back to touring. In 2002, he released the album *There and Back Again*. Over the next few years, he continued to tour and produce albums. Phil Lesh and Friends found success among their fans—mainly Deadheads and newcomers.

In 2003, Phil Lesh joined fellow Grateful Dead members Bob Weir, Bill Kreutzmann, and Mickey Hart to form the Dead. They didn't use the name Grateful Dead out of respect for Jerry Garcia. At these concerts, Deadheads and many new fans come out to hear and watch them play. The younger fans were introduced to the music by their parents.

In 2005, Phil Lesh's memoir *Searching for the Sound—My Life With the Grateful Dead* was published. The book made the *New York Times* Best Seller List. In the fall of 2006, Image Entertainment released Phil Lesh and Friends' first DVD. It is titled *Live at the Warfield*.

Unfortunately, in 2006, Lesh's prostrate cancer returned. He underwent surgery at the end of that year. As a cancer survivor and because he received a liver transplant from a donor, Lesh created the Unbroken Chain Foundation, a volunteer organization that hosts musical events to raise money for worthwhile nonprofit organizations. Phil Lesh is married; he and his wife, Jill, have two sons.

Mickey Hart

Mickey Hart's passion for world music sparked his interest in many charities. This passion actually started at Grateful Dead shows, when he and fellow drummer Bill Kreutzmann introduced new percussion instruments to their fans. Here his interest in world music, sounds from around the globe, started to grow. He wanted to hear more, and that hunger caused him to travel around the world. In 1996, Hart gathered one hundred percussionists to perform music he wrote at the opening ceremony at the Centennial Olympic Games.

Hart is known as an ethnomusicologist, a person who studies music from around the world. He performs, records, and produces indigenous musical traditions often working with well-known musicians from around the world. In 1991, his album *Planet Drum* hit the number one spot on the Billboard World Music Chart. It remained there for twenty-six weeks. *Planet Drum* also received the Grammy for Best World Music Album in 1991. It was the first Grammy awarded in this category. *Planet Drum* is one of thirty-three recordings released on Hart's World Series label under the Rykodisc label. Under his World Series label, Hart's music covers sounds from as far away as Papua New Guinea and Bali in

Indonesia. He founded the Endangered Music Fund in 2002. His goals for the Endangered Music Fund are to return royalty payments from many of the recordings on the World Series label to the indigenous people that created them and to further the preservation of sounds and music from around the world.

In a June 6, 2003, interview, Hart said his love of world music began as "a fortunate accident." "My mom inherited a wonderful collection of Count Basie and Duke Ellington records and for some reason, stuck somewhere in the middle of that shelf, was a strange album—these magnificent sounds of African Pygmies. It lit my imagination, suggested possibilities, and opened a strange new world to a kid growing up in the city. I had access to their daily lives, their experiences, and their essence. My mind went wild with the possibilities."[5]

Mickey Hart (right) drums and dances with demonstrators in California in 1997.

While playing with the Grateful Dead, Phil Lesh gave Hart a recording called “Drums of North and South India.” While he listened, he was amazed to learn that there was “a whole world of indigenous music out there,” he said. “I knew at that time, all of these musicians, all of this music, should be recorded with the same kind of equipment, the same kind of technology and the same passion as the Grateful Dead is being recorded.”[6]

In addition to recording albums and performing in concerts, Hart composed scores, sound tracks, and themes for movies and television, including *Apocalypse Now*, *Gang Related*, *Hearts of Darkness*, *The Twilight Zone*, the 1987 score to *The America's Cup: The Walter Cronkite Report*, *Vietnam: A Television History*, and *The Next Step*. He got the opportunity to write the music for the anti-Vietnam War movie *Apocalypse Now* when he was approached by movie director Francis Ford Coppola. Coppola went to a Rhythm Devils concert and asked Hart to compose the percussive score.

Hart also loves history and mythology. That combined with music led him to write four books: *Drumming at the Edge of Magic*, *Planet Drum*, *Spirit Into Sound: The Magic of Music*, and *Songcatchers: In Search of the World's Music*.

Hart's love of music has also led him to become a social activist. In 1991, he addressed the U.S. Senate Committee on the healing values of drumming and music. Hart strongly believes that music has a beneficial effect on the afflictions associated with aging. He joined the Institute for Music and Neurologic Function at Beth Abraham Hospital in the Bronx, New York, in 2000. Doctors and researchers at Beth Abraham Hospital have found that music can help patients with Alzheimer's disease, Parkinson's disease, depression, and those recovering from strokes. Music therapy unlocks memories, helps with coordination, and boosts self-esteem.

Hart is also a board member at the American Folklife Center at the Library of Congress. He heads the subcommittee on the digitization and preservation of the center's vast collections. These collections include Thomas Edison's wax-cylinder recording machine, invented in 1877, and the latest digital audio equipment, which records the voices and music of many regional, ethnic, and cultural groups.

In October 2000, Hart received an honorary doctorate of humane letters from the Saybrook Graduate School and Research Center in San Francisco for his work on preserving and promoting world music. Sharing his love of world music is an integral part of his life. Hart continues to write music, tour with the Mickey Hart Band, and perform with Bill Kreutzmann as one half of the Rhythm Devils. Hart lives in Sonoma County in California and performs as part of the Rhythm Devils and his own band called the Mickey Hart Band.

Bill Kreutzmann

When the Grateful Dead came to an end, Kreutzmann retired to Hawaii. His retirement was brief. He appeared on an album with blues-rock band Backbone and released a CD in 1998. Two years later, he was on the road touring with the Other Ones, a rock band comprised of former Dead musicians Bob Weir, Mickey Hart, and Bruce Hornsby, and musicians Steve Kimock, Mark Karan, and Alphonso Johnson.

Kreutzmann started a second career as a digital artist. He loves the immediacy of digital art and likens it to the spontaneous experience of drumming.

He produces a wide array of colorful digital art. Many of his creations are sold at galleries and on his Web site.

Kreutzmann lives with his family in Hawaii. He has a farm where he grows pineapple, different varieties of lettuce, and flowers. On occasion, he continues to create art and music and tour. He keeps in touch with former Grateful Dead members, including Robert Hunter, who also wrote music for the Other Ones. He still tours with the Rhythm Devils. His son, Justin Kreutzmann, is a documentary filmmaker.

Robert Hunter

Robert Hunter released the solo album *Tales of the Great Rum Runners* in 1974. It features him as a singer and songwriter. It was followed the next year by *Tiger Rose*. He gives solo performances in California and other parts of the country and still writes lyrics for Ratdog, Phil Lesh and Friends, and other musicians such as Bob Dylan and Jefferson Starship. He and his family live in California.

Tom Constanten

In the early 1990s, Tom Constanten released an album of classical sonatas and another two albums mixing original material with a few Dead songs. One album titled *Dead Ringers* is composed of Grateful Dead, Bob Dylan, and other songs. In 1993, Constanten married Beth Diggs. Their daughter, Clarissa Lee, was born in 1997. Constanten and his family live in North Carolina.

Of the five Grateful Dead keyboardists, Constanten is the only one that is still alive. Many Deadheads believed the keyboardist position was a jinxed gig. Today, Constanten still plays keyboard. He tours with Jefferson Starship, a rock band that was popular in the 1970s and 1980s. He was inducted into the Rock and Roll Hall of Fame in 1994.

Donna Jean Godchaux MacKay

A native of Muscle Shoals, Alabama, Donna Jean Godchaux MacKay was inducted into the Alabama Music Hall of Fame. In the late 1990s, she toured with her husband in the Donna Jean Band. She also performs with the Heart of Gold Band. In 2004, Heart of Gold released a CD called *At the Table*, a collection of original songs by Brian Godchaux (brother of

Keith Godchaux), Donna Jean Godchaux MacKay, Zion Rock Godchaux (her son with Keith), David MacKay (her husband), and Kinsman MacKay (her son with David). The music is a mixture of electric and acoustic roots with electric violin and mandolin. Most recently, she joined a group called the Tricksters, which morphed into Donna Jean and the Tricksters. The music, much like the Grateful Dead, focuses on

In 2007, Donna Jean Godchaux MacKay performs with Dark Star Orchestra in Connecticut.

jamming, bluegrass, blues, folk, and rock. In the late 1990s, she formed the Donna Jean Band with her husband, Dave MacKay, and her son Zion, who plays rhythm guitar and percussion.

Donna Jean Godchaux MacKay, Jerry Garcia, Bob Weir, Phil Lesh, Mickey Hart, Bill Kreutzmann, Robert Hunter, and Tom Constanten were inducted into the Rock and Roll Hall of Fame on January 19, 1994. Keith Godchaux, Ron "Pigpen" McKernan, Brent Mydland, and Vince Welnick were inducted into the Rock and Roll Hall of Fame that same year posthumously. Part-time Grateful Dead member Bruce Hornsby presented the awards to his friends at the Rock and Roll Hall of Fame.

The Music Lives On

On February 10, 2007, the Grateful Dead received the Lifetime Achievement Award at the Grammys. This special award is given to musicians who have made outstanding contributions in their musical fields. Hart and Kreutzmann accepted the award on behalf of the band.

Also in 2007, forty years after the formation of the Grateful Dead, fans gathered at an auction in hopes of obtaining Grateful Dead memorabilia. Bidders paid more than $1.1 million for various artifacts that belonged to members of the Grateful Dead. Jerry Garcia's cream-colored 1975 Travis Bean electric guitar brought in $312,000. Other guitars,

FROM LEFT TO RIGHT: PHIL LESH, BILL KREUTZMANN, BOB WEIR, AND MICKEY HART PERFORMED TOGETHER IN 2002 DURING A GRATEFUL DEAD REUNION CONCERT.

formerly owned by Garcia, were on the auction block at Bonhams & Butterfields in San Francisco. A fan paid $102,000 for an acoustic guitar and $39,000 for a Gibson electric. One of Garcia's leather guitar straps sold for $20,400—four times its initial asking price. Garcia's flight case, which was filled with guitar picks, strings, and other accessories, sold for $16,800.[7]

Also in May 2007, Lee Johnson, a classical composer, created the symphony *Dead Symphony No. 6: An Orchestral Tribute to the Grateful Dead*. Johnson arranged about a dozen Grateful Dead songs for the symphony, which was performed by the Russian National Orchestra. Members of the Grateful Dead were flattered. "The music of the Grateful Dead was complex, with intertwining themes of rhythm and melody, rich harmonic development and explosive dynamics; the same stuff one finds in classical music," Weir said.[8]

That complexity of their music intrigued professors at the University of Massachusetts at Amherst enough to teach a course called The Grateful Dead and American Culture. The course explores the history of the time of the 1960s and 1970s, American culture, and the Grateful Dead's music through workshops, exhibits, and performances.

Fans have long understood the complexity and simplicity of the Grateful Dead's music. "You can listen to a Grateful Dead song so many times and never tire of it," says Cub. "On the surface—when you first listen—the tunes are simple and easy to enjoy. At the same time, when you listen over and over again, you hear how complex and wonderful they are."[9]

The producers at SIRIUS Satellite Radio agree. SIRIUS Satellite Radio has launched a twenty-four-hour Grateful Dead radio channel dedicated to the music of the Grateful Dead and its band members.

Grateful Dead members are keeping the music and the memories alive by playing Grateful Dead songs at their concerts. Fans have a library of ninety-four Grateful Dead albums to listen to—many are recordings from concerts. The old music and new songs from former members continue to spark interest among fans.

Jerry Garcia once said, "We need magic, and bliss, and power, myth, and celebration and religion in our lives, and music is a good way to encapsulate a lot of it."[10]

Like the song "Truckin'" says, it really has been "a long strange trip" for the members of the band and their fans. For all of the members of the Grateful Dead and their fans, the music lives on.

TIMELINE

1965—Grateful Dead is founded in San Francisco, California, in December.

1966—The band performs in their first New Year's Eve concert at the Fillmore in San Francisco; the Grateful Dead signs with Warner Bros. (records); the Grateful Dead releases its first album called *The Grateful Dead*; Mickey Hart joins the band at the end of September.

1968—Tom Constanten joins the band on keyboards.

1969—The Grateful Dead plays at Woodstock.

1970—Tom Constanten leaves the band; The Grateful Dead takes its first concert tour in England; Grateful Dead forms own record label called Ice Nine.

1971—Keith and Donna Godchaux join the band.

1972—Ron "Pigpen" McKernan leaves the band due to declining health.

1973—Ron "Pigpen" McKernan dies in Corte Madera, California, at age twenty-seven; seven hundred fifty thousand people attend the Watkins Glen concert.

1977—*The Grateful Dead* movie is released to rave reviews.

1978—The band appears on the television show *Saturday Night Live.*

1979—Keith and Donna Godchaux leave the band; Brent Mydland joins the band.

1980—Keith Godchaux dies in a car accident in Marin County, California, at age thirty-two.

1986—Jerry Garcia lapses into a near-fatal diabetic coma for five days; the Grateful Dead returns to performing five months after Garcia emerges from a coma.

1987—The album *In the Dark* lands on Billboard Magazine's Top Ten list.

1990—Brent Mydland dies of a drug overdose in Lafayette, California, at age thirty-seven; Vince Welnick joins the band on keyboards; Bruce Hornsby joins the band as a regular guest on keyboards.

1991—Grateful Dead Comix are published.

1992—Bruce Hornsby leaves the band; Jerry Garcia collapses from exhaustion and cancels a tour.

1994—Members of the Grateful Dead are inducted into the Rock and Roll Hall of Fame.

1995—The last Grateful Dead show is held at Soldier Field; Jerry Garcia dies at age fifty-three; in December, the remaining members of the Grateful Dead decide to dissolve the band out of respect for Jerry Garcia.

2003—The band the Dead is formed by former members of the Grateful Dead; members of the band continue to tour and perform together. They all have their own bands.

2007—The Grateful Dead receives Lifetime Achievement Award at the Grammys.

DISCOGRAPHY

1967 *The Grateful Dead*

1968 *Anthem of the Sun*

1969 *Aoxomoxoa*

Live Dead

1970 *Workingman's Dead*

American Beauty

1971 *Grateful Dead* (also known as *Skull and Roses*)

1972 *Europe '72*

1973 *History of the Grateful Dead, Volume One Wake of the Flood*

1974 *Grateful Dead from the Mars Hotel*

1975 *Blues for Allah*

1976 *Steal Your Face*

1977 *Terrapin Station*

1978 *Shakedown Street*

1980 *Go to Heaven*

1981 *Reckoning*

Dead Set

1987 *In the Dark*

1988 *Dylan and the Dead*

1989 *Built to Last*

1990 *Without a Net*

1991 *Infrared Roses*

1999 *So Many Roads* (1965–1995)

2001 *The Golden Road* (1965–1973)

2002 *Postcards of the Hanging*

2003 *Birth of the Dead*

2004 *Beyond Description*

2005 *Rare Cuts and Oddities 1966*

COMPILATION/BOX SETS

1974 *Skeletons from the Closet: The Best of the Grateful Dead*

1977 *What a Long Strange Trip It's Been*

1987 *Dead Zone: The Grateful Dead CD Collection (1977–1987)*

1996 *The Arista Years*

1997 *Selections from the Arista Years*

1999 *So Many Roads (1965–1995) Sampler*

2001 *The Golden Road (1965–1973)*

2003 *The Very Best of the Grateful Dead*

2004 *Beyond Description (1973–1989)*

2005 *The Complete Fillmore West 1969*

RETROSPECTIVE LIVE ALBUMS

From *One From the Vault, 1991, to Live at the Cow Palace*, 2007, the Grateful Dead produced twenty-seven retrospective live albums.

Dick's Picks—Dick Latvala, the Grateful Dead's archivist, put together thirty-six albums of music from various Grateful Dead concerts.

Concert Tours

The Grateful Dead was known as a touring band. They toured throughout the United States from 1965 through 1995. They also performed in Canada, Europe, and Egypt.

1965–1966	*The Matrix*
1966	*Trips Festival*
1969	*Family Dog*
1967	*The Great Human Be-In*
	Monterey Pop Festival
	Expo 67
1969	*Woodstock Festival*
1972	*Steppin' Out with the Grateful Dead European Tour*
	Farewell Series
1986	*The Dead tour with Bob Dylan and Tom Petty*
	The Dead tour with Bob Dylan
1988	*Bruce Hornsby opens for and jams with Grateful Dead*
1995	*Tour From Hell*

GLOSSARY

bluegrass—An American style of music that was inspired by Irish, English, and Scottish immigrant musicians.

blues-rock—A style of music that combines elements of the blues with rock and roll and places a lot of emphasis on the electric guitar.

Deadheads—Fans of the Grateful Dead who attend the majority of their concerts.

ethnomusicologist—A person who studies music from around the world.

folk—A musical genre that combines folk music with rock and roll.

jamming—A form of musical improvisation that often includes long musical numbers.

lyricist—Someone who writes the words of a song.

memorabilia—Objects that are kept or collected because of their association with memorable people, places, or things.

psychedelic rock—A style of rock and roll that is inspired by experiences brought on by mind-altering drugs.

record—A vinyl disc with spiral grooves on which sound is recorded. Records are played on record players. They are also called LPs or 45s, depending on the size of the disc.

world music—Music from all over of the globe.

Chapter Notes

Chapter 1. Really Grateful

1. Personal interview with Jane Healy, November 9, 2006.

2. Ibid.

3. Dennis McNally, *A Long Strange Trip—The Inside History of the Grateful Dead* (New York: Broadway Books, 2002), p. 457.

4. Personal interview with Dennis McNally, November 30, 2006.

Chapter 2. A Band Without a Leader

1. Personal interview with Bob Weir, March 30, 2007.

2. Personal interview with Dennis McNally, November 30, 2006.

3. Ibid.

4. "Jerry Garcia: Biography," Answers.com, n.d., <http://www.answers.com/Jerry+Garcia+quotes?cat=entertainment> (July 17, 2007).

5. Ibid.

6. Ibid.

7. Mary Eisenhart, "Jerry Garcia Interview," November 12, 1987, <http://www.yoyow.com/marye/garcia.html> (October 10, 2007).

8. Blair Jackson, *Garcia: An American Life* (New York: Viking, 1999), p. 333.

9. Personal interview with Bob Weir, March 30, 2007.

10. Ibid.

11. Ibid.

12. Ibid.

13. Ibid.

14. Personal interview with Dennis McNally, November 30, 2006.

15. Sarah Bruner, "Just a Guy Who Plays the Drums: An Interview with Bill Kreutzmann," January 31, 1999, <http://www.jambands.com/mar99/features/kreutzmann.html> (October 10, 2007).

16. "Grateful Dead Ends Its 'Long, Strange Trip,'" CNN.com, December 9, 1995, <http://www.cnn.com/SHOWBIZ/Music/9512/grateful_dead/index.html> (October 4, 2007).

17. Alan Sculley, "Mickey Hart Returns with New Band, New CD," n.d., <http://www.metroactive.com/papers/sonoma/09.03.98/mickeyhart-9835.html> (October 10, 2007).

18. Personal interview with Dennis McNally, November 30, 2006.

19. "Biography: Bruce Hornsby," Brucehornsby.com, n.d., <http://www.brucehornsby.com/bio.htm> (July 17, 2007).

20. Ibid.

Chapter 3. History of the Band

1. Personal interview with Bob Weir, March 30, 2007.

2. Ibid.

3. Greg Kot, "Ever Grateful," *Chicago Tribune*, August 13, 1995, p. 12.

4. Robert Christgau, "The Dead in Four Dimensions," *Village Voice*, June 13, 1977, p. 51.

Chapter 4. Famous Songs and Concerts

1. "On the Road," Mickey Hart interview, n.d., <http://kazart.com/bus_stop/switch1.htm> (March 24, 2008).

2. Personal interview with Dennis McNally, November 27, 2007.

3. Ibid.

Chapter 5. Deadheads

1. Personal interview with Jane Healy, November 9, 2006.

2. Ibid.

3. Ibid.

4. Personal interview with Bob Weir, March 30, 2007.

5. Personal interview with John "Cub" Ganrahan, November 10, 2006.

6. Ibid.

7. Ibid.

8. Personal interview with Jane Healy, November 9, 2006.

9. Ibid.

10. Personal interview with John "Cub" Ganrahan, November 10, 2006.

11. Ibid.

12. Ibid.

13. Ibid.

14. Ibid.

15. Personal interview with Megan McWilliams, March 27, 2007.

16. Ibid.

17. Ibid.

18. Personal interview with Justin Ben-Asher, April 16, 2007.

19. Ibid.

20. Ibid.

21. Personal interview with David Gans, April 25, 2007.

22. Ibid.

23. "Interview with Phil Lesh," Dead to the World on KPFA 94.1 FM, David Gans, host, April 2, 2007, <http://www.levity.com/gans/Lesh.970402.html> (October 4, 2007).

Chapter 6. The World Around Them: 1960s–1990s

1. Personal interview with Dennis McNally, December 10, 2006.

2. Dick Nesser, "Plenty of Life in Grateful Dead," *Billboard*, June 11, 1977, p. 38.

3. Ibid.

4. Ibid.

Chapter 7. Honoring Jerry Garcia

1. Dave White, "CD Review Garcia Plays Dylan," About.com, n.d., <http://classicrock.about.com/od/cdandconcertreviews/fr/garcia_dylan.htm> (July 17, 2007).

2. Andrew Ferguson, "The Gimlet Eye-Overblown Rhetoric Attending Guitarist Jerry Garcia's Death," *National Review*, September 11, 1995, <http://findarticles.com/p/articles/mi_m1282/is_n17_v47/ai_17374473> (October 4, 2007).

3. Personal interview John "Cub" Ganrahan, November 13, 2006.

4. Ibid.

5. Personal interview with Dennis McNally, December 10, 2006.

6. Ibid.

7. Mary Eisenhart, "Jerry Garcia Interview," *BAM Magazine*, November 12, 1987.

8. Ibid.

9. Dan Aquilante, "Phish-Er Isn't One to Carp," *New York Post*, January 1, 1999, p. 32.

10. Jerry Garcia, ThinkExist.com, n.d., <http://thinkexist.com/quote/jerry_garcia/> (October 10, 2007).

Chapter 8. Where Are They Now?

1. Personal interview with Bob Weir, March 30, 2007.

2. Ibid.

3. Ibid.

4. Ibid.

5. Brian Handwerk, "Q&A: Mickey Hart on New Songcatchers Book," *National Geographic News*, June 6, 2003, <http://news.nationalgeographic.com/news/2003/06/0605_030606_mickeyhartqa.html> (October 4, 2007).

6. Ibid.

7. Steve Ruberstein, "Top dollar for Dead's Skeletons: Grateful fans bid on road manager's memorabilia to tune of $1.1 million," *San Francisco Chronicle*, May 9, 2007, <http://sfgate.com/cgi-bin/article.cgi?f=/c/a/2007/05/09/BAGGJPNHGL1.DTL> (October 4, 2007).

8. John Rogers, "Grateful Dead Goes Symphonic," *TheLedger.com*, June 29, 2007, <http://theledger.com/

article/20070629/NEWS/706290356/1021/LIFE> (August 15, 2007).

9. Personal interview with John "Cub" Ganrahan, November 13, 2006.

10. Blair Jackson, *Garcia: An American Life* (New York: Viking, 1999), p. 474.

Further Reading

Books

Blakesburg, Jay. *Between the Dark and Light: The Grateful Dead Photography of Jay Blakesburg*. San Francisco, Calif.: Backbeat Books, 2002.

Garcia, Jerry, and David Grisman. *The Teddy Bears' Picnic*. New York: HarperCollins, 1996.

Hayes, Malcolm. *1970s: Turbulent Times*. Milwaukee, Wisc.: Gareth Stevens, 2002.

Herald, Jacqueline. *Fashions of a Decade: The 1970s*. New York: Facts on File, 2006.

Kallen, Stuart A. *The Instruments of Music*. San Diego, Calif.: Lucent Books, 2003.

McIntosh, Kenneth. *The Grateful Dead*. Broomfall, Pa.: Mason Crest Publishers, 2007.

Piccoli, Sean. *The Grateful Dead*. Philadelphia, Pa.: Chelsea House Publishers, 1997.

Internet Addresses

Grateful Dead

<http://cla.calpoly.edu/Cla/legacies/dbsmith/dbsmithsite/519Stu98/MikePock/main.html>

Grateful Dead

<http://www.dead.net/>

INDEX

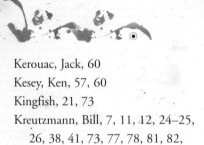